OUT OF ARCADIA

Pan by K.S. Roy

OUT OF ARCADIA

A Devotional Anthology in Honor of Pan

Edited by Diotima Sophia

Foreword by Richard Derks

Copyright © 2011 by Neos Alexandria

All rights reserved. No part of this book may be reproduced by any means or in any form whatsoever without written permission from the author(s), except for brief quotations embodied in literary articles or reviews. Copyright reverts to individual authors after publication.

Dedication: Homeric Hymn XIX (To Pan)

Translated by H.G. Evelyn-White

(ll. 1-26) Muse, tell me about Pan, the dear son of Hermes, with his goat's feet and two horns -- a lover of merry noise. Through wooded glades he wanders with dancing nymphs who foot it on some sheer cliff's edge, calling upon Pan, the shepherd-god, long-haired, unkempt. He has every snowy crest and the mountain peaks and rocky crests for his domain; hither and thither he goes through the close thickets, now lured by soft streams, and now he presses on amongst towering crags and climbs up to the highest peak that overlooks the flocks. Often he courses through the glistening high mountains, and often on the shouldered hills he speeds along slaying wild beasts, this keen-eyed god. Only at evening, as he returns from the chase, he sounds his note, playing sweet and low on his pipes of reed: not even she could excel him in melody -- that bird who in flower-laden spring pouring forth her lament utters honey-voiced song amid the leaves. At that hour the clear-voiced nymphs are with him and move with nimble feet, singing by some spring of dark water, while Echo wails about the mountain-top, and the god on this side or on that of the choirs, or at times sidling into the midst, plies it nimbly with his feet. On his back he wears a spotted lynx-pelt, and he delights in high-pitched songs in a soft meadow where crocuses and sweet-smelling hyacinths bloom at random in the grass.

(ll. 27-47) They sing of the blessed gods and high Olympus and choose to tell of such a one as luck-bringing Hermes above the rest, how he is the swift messenger of all the gods, and how he came to Arcadia, the land of many springs and mother of flocks, there where his sacred place is as god of Cyllene. For there, though a god, he used to tend curly-fleeced sheep in the service of a mortal man, because there fell on him and waxed strong melting desire to wed the rich-tressed daughter of Dryops, and there be brought about the merry marriage. And in the house she bare Hermes a dear son who from his birth was marvellous to look upon, with goat's feet and two horns -- a noisy, merry-laughing child. But when the nurse saw his uncouth face and full beard, she was afraid and sprang up and fled and left the child. Then luck-bringing Hermes received him and took him in his arms: very glad in his heart was the god. And he went quickly to the abodes of the deathless gods, carrying the son wrapped in warm skins of mountain hares, and set him down beside Zeus and showed him to the rest of the gods. Then all the immortals were glad in heart and Bacchic Dionysus in especial; and they called the boy Pan because he delighted all their hearts.

(ll. 48-49) And so hail to you, lord! I seek your favour with a song. And now I will remember you and another song also.

Table of Contents

Dedication: Homeric Hymn XIX (To Pan) v
Foreword by Richard Derks ix
Acknowledgments xi
Introduction xii
Pan Agrios 1
   Kenn Payne
Aegipan 2
   P. Sufenas Virius Lupus
Ancient God 4
   Diotima Sophia
Pan-ic! 5
   Kenn Payne
Hymn to Pan I 7
   Rebecca Buchanan
Arcadia's Doors 8
   Diotima Sophia
Homage to Pan 9
   Galina Krasskova
Pan the Initiator 11
   Leafshimmer
Pan's Arrivals: Epiphanies and Invocations in Modern Literature
   and Lyric 16
   Michael Routery
Panantinous 22
   P. Sufenas Virius Lupus
Bargain 24
   Diotima Sophia
Hymn to Pan II 25
   Rebecca Buchanan
Wild Beauty 26
   Tabitha Few
To Goat-Footed Pan 27
   Amanda Sioux Blake
Thundering Pan 28
   Diana Rajchel

Pan and the Feminist Consciousness 29
    Diotima Sophia
Hymn to Pan III 35
    Rebecca Buchanan
The Horns of a Dilemma: Beltane and SexGnosis as a "Research
    Method" 36
    Dr Dave Evans
Pan's Mistakes 43
    P. Sufenas Virius Lupus
From a Distance 44
    Diotima Sophia
Hymn to Pan IV 49
    Rebecca Buchanan
Dithyramb for Pan 50
    Christa A. Bergerson
God Crush 53
    Jason Ross Inczauskis
You Press 56
    Diotima Sophia
Pan 57
    Michael Routery
Hymn to Pan V 58
    Rebecca Buchanan
Io Pan! 59
    Kenn Payne
Reports of My Death 61
    Diotima Sophia
The Piper of the Big Wood 66
    Rebecca Buchanan
From Arcadia With Love: Pan and the Cult of Antinous 86
    P. Sufenas Virius Lupus
Lament at Banias 94
    Diotima Sophia

Author Biographies 96
Select Bibliography 100
About the Bibliotheca Alexandrina 103

Foreword

I've always had a soft spot for Pan, because he was my first. Pan was the first Hellenic Deity that I was introduced to, incidentally when I was a child. I daresay many of us started our fascination with the classical Gods through an infatuation with Pan. He has a sort of inviting and playful countenance about him that is in stark contrast to the stricter and often more authoritative Gods that most of us are exposed to in our early lives. In my own case he was introduced to me through a lesson from my first grade teacher. I still remember sitting at a table while she played a film strip (remember those?), and the little ditty that accompanied it: "Pan, Pan, the Greek God Pan. One half goat, the other half man." She then proceeded to tell a tale that would stay with me for the rest of my life and influence how I myself approach the Gods to this day.

In her tale she described how a boy was asked to sacrifice his favorite goat as an offering to Pan. He didn't want to because he loved the goat so much, but she then explained how only the offering of something meaningful, something which you love or which you have imbued with your own time, effort, and toil is truly a gift worthy of sacrifice. For some reason this concept really struck me and ignited within me the first spark that would kindle into a true love of the old gods that would eventually lead me to their worship some many years later. I assume this was not the effect my first grade teacher was hoping to have, but Pan had other plans, and he tends to get his way, as the mythology surrounding him will verify.

Looking through the contents of this book that you now hold in your hands I can say that by the criteria expanded upon above, it is a proper and fitting offering to goat-footed God. The time and effort that have gone into the individual author contributions is evident, the love and devotion is without question. If offerings of meaning and sacrifice are what Pan truly desires, then I daresay that I think he would be pleased. Pan, among other things, is a God of passion and I do say that his passion is met with like kind within these pages.

Pan is a figure who has captured the imagination of man throughout the ages. You will find his likeness in statues, in literary works of fiction, movies, even commercials. Seldom in these sources however will you hear about him from the perspective of those who actually love him, those who sing his name in praise out of love and true devotion, and not just a purely intellectual interest. Oftentimes, learning about a particular divinity can be difficult. You may have many scholarly resources available to you, but these don't tell you what it is like to really *know* the God, to be a devotee of them, to interact with them or worship them on a daily basis. That is where a book like this truly excels, and it is the main reason I am a fan of the Bibliotheca Alexandrina devotional titles. The passion of the voices that make up the anthology tells a story of what it is to truly worship these Gods in a way that is very real and honest, and in a way you will be hard pressed to find elsewhere.

In this devotional you will hear many voices raised in praise of Pan. Once more his name finds its way into poetry, not as a quaint rustic Deity some ancient civilization once believed in, but in true praise and devotion fitting of a very real and living God. Inside you will find personal accounts of interactions with him, poetry, prayers, and scholarly essays that explain his origins and compare him to other horned Gods. In short, through the voices contained within, you will learn about him from those who love him best — and who better to learn from?

Io Pan!

[An Ovate in the Order of Bards, Ovates and Druids, and a Druid Apprentice in the Ancient Order of Druids in America, Richard Derks is particularly devoted to Hekate and The Horned God. He maintains the site *The Serpents Wisdom*, and is the editor of *Hoofprints in the Wildwood: A Devotional for Cernunnos* (Gullinbursti Press).]

Acknowledgments

The editor would like to thank Allyson Szabo and Rebecca Buchanan for their help in editing this work, and the members of Neos Alexandria for their input. There is obviously also a debt of thanks to those who contributed to the work.

And, as always, I would wish to thank my family and friends for their support, conversation and input.

Introduction

Pan always seems to be around. He was well known to our ancestors, he appears in medieval and Renaissance Western art, in Victorian poetry and novels, in modern film and media. At times, he takes a side place, as in the ancient temples where only his face appears in corners, or he follows the titular deity in procession. At other times, he takes centre stage as of right, claiming our attention for his own.

Perhaps echoing the best known view of his parentage, Pan is a mercurial god. We know him best as a bringer of music, a reveller in dance and lust. But he can also be a god of anger and terror – panic, after all, takes its name from Pan's means of attack. Yet he was also honoured as a healing god, who brought health in dreams. He is nothing if not multifaceted.

The works in this anthology do not capture the essence of Pan, any more than a snapshot carried in a wallet captures the essence of a loved one. The photo may tell you about the eye and hair colour, it may capture an expression or show beauty of bone structure, But it does not – cannot – adequately express what it is about that person which incites you to carry their picture around. The poems, stories and essays in the present work are much the same; they show us facets of Pan, as seen through the eyes of a diverse group of people.

We see him in the American heartland, we hear his call at his ancient cult centre, we encounter him in modern ritual and see his effect on men and women, even investigate the intersection between honouring the god and a modern equality movement. The works in this slim volume look to the past as well as to the present, and lay a foundation for the future.

I won't way that there has been a revival of interest in Pan, because that interest has always been there, bubbling along, adding element of eroticism, music and dream to even the most ordered and modern of societies.

This anthology is an offering to the Great God Pan – our world might be the better for his gifts.

Diotima Sophia, England, 2010

Pan Agrios

Kenn Payne

Pan! Pan!

Wild goat-man!

Play the pipes in wooded dells

Hell-like terror starts to swell.

Shadows lengthen; your canopies hide the sun.

Filled with Your panic –

Where to run?

Hoof and horn hide in the gloom,

For the careless traveller Your presence like doom.

Haunting-lyrical is Your song,

Through fear and change can we belong –

To Your Freedom!

Aegipan

P. Sufenas Virius Lupus

As a constellation of stars the goat
that is part fish from dark of night watches,
ever-waiting in case his skill again
needs come to aid of gods with might and men.

Foster-brother of Zeus, lightning-flinging,
they sucked at teats of goat hidden in cave;
dancer, Aegipan taught to Kouretes
the dance of beating shields to cause panic.

He taught the gods to hide away in forms
of animals when Typhon terrible
savaged the earth and stole most stealthily
the very sinews of thundering Zeus.

As a sea creature he stockpiled shellfish
and with speed blinding and dexterity
by Hermes' swift side the two gods retrieved
the sinews and restored them to great Zeus.

He invited Typhon to a fine feast
of fish on the seashore sumptuously
and Titans and giants accompanied
where the trap was laid in wait for monsters.

A rain of fish, eels, angry octopi,
dolphins, rays, sharks, and a barrage of shells
hurled by Aegipan assaulted giants
on the strand where the feast had just begun.

Surging sea swelled as Aegipan's allies
doubled their efforts, brought breakers' horses

down on enemies, Nerites' kingdom
assaulting with calcium-hard harshness.

Typhon, confused, raging, did not see Zeus
as he hurled his weapon from stormy sky,
an eagle for quickness, death from above,
shattered Typhon's power forever then.

In Aetna he sleeps imprisoned in stone;
Zeus and the gods delight in victory,
from Egypt as animals they return,
and Aegipan's reward is bright heavens.

Ancient God ....

Diotima Sophia

They say on Mainalos
    You can hear the piper play
The flute sounds soft in the evening breeze
    Heard at the close of day

Among the oldest gods is he
    the shepherd of the land
The oak stands by – his sacred tree
    As healing comes from the hand

Of Pan Skoleita, Pan of the Lykain games
    Pan the hunter, Pan the satyr
    Pan – of a thousand names

Erato was his prophet
    To give his thoughts to men

In dreams was found his healing hand
    And can be found – again.

Pan-ic!

Kenn Payne

Drumming in my temples,
Pulse behind my eyes.
Heart fluttering like a flailing bird
Sensation – mercurial fear –
Like ice through my veins
Tells me You're near.

Cold sweat prickles my brow,
You chortle from the thicket –
Shadow and fur, unseen
Unknowing...
Desire to run
But to where?

To flee –
Would You follow me?
Longing for the adrenal rush
A scare of ecstasy –
Dry mouth full of the taste of divine panic!

Hoof-falls in the gloom make
Hairs prick and skin crawl.
Fog of fear
Encroaches on the senses;
Reason long abandoned.

To continue
Explore Your power
Fear of wanting –
Wanting to change
Changing to be
Being free.

You show me the way with rustic charm.
Fear, fright, terror, panic –
To know You in these I am
Shown the way
To dance to Your pipes
As You lead me ever onward ....

Hymn to Pan I

Rebecca Buchanan

I sing of Pan

Curlybeard

Lover of Nymphs and Naiads

Piper

Dancer

The whole immortal host

Delights in your sweet sounds and skilful steps

(after an anonymous inscription found at Epidauros)

Arcadia's Doors

Diotima Sophia

Arcadia opens its doors to you:
    It urges
        And ushers
            And beckons you through

The formal and staid,
    The trite and mundane
Leave behind you as dead;
    Come – be insane!

For insanity's mine
    My gift to bestow
The Gods are not sane
    And as above – so below

For love is not logical
    Nor is it sane
Yet it conquers the strong man
    Overcomes might and mien

Insanity beckons
    Come – frolic with me!
The dark, goat-god beckons
    Hear him – or flee

Homage to Pan

Galina Krasskova

I wanted to honor You, God of wilderness and fury,
because my mother loved You;
and now that she is gone,
I find myself carefully retracing
her footsteps, so that I too might pay homage
to all the holy halls into which her heart once led.

She told me often how You had whispered to her once
in the wild preserve where she worked sometimes;
how you had tempted her to yield to the fury
that so often filled her heart, when faced with
humanity's crimes against Your holy places,
and against all the wild ones who dwell therein.
As she walked through the brush, picking up trash
so carelessly discarded without thought or sense,
she told me how she had longed to run with You,
to cast off the uneasy glamour of humanity,
which she never liked anyway.
You were the only God who might ever have tempted her
to embrace the starkness of the bacchante's frenzy,
and You needed no wine to kindle its mad rage,
only a dry whisper, the smell of wet fur, rotting, tangled roots,
and a few sinuous notes carried dancingly --
almost out of hearing -- in the crisp morning's breeze.
But she belonged to other Gods
and only that allowed her to ignore the sweetness of Your piping.

Giver of panic,
You Who kindled delight in a lonely woman's heart;
Keeper of a thousand forgotten senses,
Rutting Goat-God of the mountaintop,
of grove, and glen, and all sweet, hidden places

I too belong to other Gods,
but I will bow my head before You,
and keep the eyes and ears of my heart keen
for some small sign of Your passing,
that I may know the proper place
in which to lay offerings at Your feet.
Till then, let this be the song with which I hail You.
Hail Pan and all the places You may roam.

Pan the Initiator

Leafshimmer

Invocation:

Dread opener of the mysterious doors
Leading to universal knowledge—see,
Great son of Dryope,
The many that are come to pay their vows
With leaves about their brows!

Be still the unimaginable lodge
For solitary thinkings; such as dodge
Conception to the very bourne of heaven,
Then leave the naked brain: be still the leaven,
That spreading in this dull and clodded earth
Gives it a touch ethereal—a new birth:
Be still a symbol of immensity;
A firmament reflected in a sea;
An element filling the space between;
An unknown...

    – John Keats: *Endymion, Book I*

"[For there is Magick to be done] in order to lift burdens grievous to be borne in a world that has forgotten the holiness of the Great Horned One." – Dion Fortune, *Moon Magic*

Push the frontiers of memory as far back as I am able, and it seems as if Pan has always been there. I have a half-memory from toddler-age of waddling down to a green bank, beyond the margins of my grandmother's back yard, to where a wild meadow beckoned with the vague music of wind brushing tall reedy grasses and high-stalked wildflowers. There was a verdant green bank with water trickling below in a drowsy stream. And suddenly there was a Light that was like no other light I had ever seen, glimmering and dazzling with a tawny lustre that came from some secret place deep within the Earth.

There was a Door, where there had been no door, and it was slowly opening, and from beyond that door came a seductive music of flutes and pipes and faint silvery tinkling bells. I toddled towards that opening gateway, delighted beyond measure, for I knew in my babe's heart that here, at last, was the realm into which I had truly meant to be born. And then – then, I have no idea, but probably an adult, lacking the Sight to see what was happening, came along and brought me back firmly into the realm of Here and Now before I was able to step through that Doorway. What I remember more firmly, from the after-time, is the lure I felt as a small child for that meadow and that green bank. I kept feeling certain that there was a door there, and that that door would open. It never appeared and was never there but the hope never really died out in my heart that I would find it again someday.

Encounter with Pan, or vision of Faery? As Dolores Ashcroft-Nowicki reminds us in her excursus upon the Faery Tradition, the memory of Pan and the vision of the Lordly Ones in Their Realm are intimately related. From the experiences I myself have had, the descriptions of the fauns, satyrs, and nymphs in the old legends seem closer to the reality of the Shining Ones – call Them Alfar, Sidhe, Elves, the Gentry, the Good People or what you will – than the Victorian fancies of Andrew Lang and Arthur Rackham when it comes to Pan and His People. RJ Stewart's work on the "Earthlight" suggests a link to the life-force of our planet. RJ's teaching shows that the life-force of each individual is inextricably bound up with the spirits of the place where we live and with the greater field of energetic consciousness thriving at the heart of Earth Herself. As Above, So Below: to me, as a male Priest of the Mysteries, Pan throbs immemorially through the pulse of my own blood through my veins, through the movement of breath in and out of my lungs, and in the mysterious thrum of my own hard-on. Io Pan! Evohe!

When I began fully to come into my own as a Pagan Priest in the late 1990s, it was Pan who led me onwards most vigorously, beautifully, and unfailingly. He came, as of old, a leaping flame, beckoning me onwards in my quest, with the allure of His laughing eyes, the seductive half-heard echo from the melody of His syrinx, the sensuous promise of His furry haunches, the flame-warm hint of His breath at my ear ever singing in His hoarsely shivering whisper Come away, come away... By Imbolc of 1999 I had Otter Zell's Pan statue on my altar; the closest thing I could find for a visual symbol of the Pan of my visions, a virile, kinetic figure of song and mirth and sexual joy. Through Him I found a deepened connection to the greenwood, to my own sensuality, even to the freedom, so long denied me, to celebrate my own naked body with other men. He was in every way an Initiatory guide — and goad — in my sacred quest. I think a similar role for some women seekers is played by Artemis/Diana, one of the Goddesses with Whom He was specially connected in Antiquity (on the Boston krater, Pan and Daphnis frolic on one side while Artemis watches the savaging of Aktaion by his own hounds on the other side — to me, these are twinned faces of the Initiatory challenge and crisis).

When I first really opened the Door of my own heart to Him, I quickly realized that Pan had always been nearby. A few furtive notes and phrases of His transfiguring Music often came welling up through the blur and clash of life as I grew and flourished into adulthood. As a boy reading "Piper at the Gates of Dawn" in *The Wind in the Willows*, or later on Plato's vision of the prayer of Socrates to Pan in the *Phaedrus*. My fascination with old photographs of Nijinsky in the *Afternoon of a Faun* ballet, and seeing Nureyev re-create (if not actively channel) the role in the Seventies on a Great Performances broadcast. The strangely compelling echo of the pan-pipes played by Zamfir in the film *Picnic at Hanging Rock*. Going further back and recalling the descriptions of Peter Pan's "cruel beautiful mouth," strangely white teeth, and uncanny laughter in the original J. M. Barrie novel. Once I started to think about it, it seemed as if Pan had been as ubiquitous as His Name would imply — although I now prefer Borgeaud's explication (citing Edwin Brown) of Pan as related to ancient Arcadian Paon, the Shepherd.

Leafing through the images collected by Hans Walter in his book *Pans Wiederkehr: der Gott der griechischen Wildnis* ("Pan's Return: the God of the Greek Wilderness") (1980), I am particularly struck by the repeated image found on various vase paintings of Pan dancing before the anodos (epiphany or birth) of Aphrodite. The God of Lust Unbridled calls forth the Goddess of Love Triumphant. The only hint I can recall of a possibility of Pan's presence at the birth of the Love Goddess comes in the texts which describe Eros (regarded as Her son in the later sources) among those who came to greet and serve the Lady upon Her arrival dancing over the foaming waves before the beach at Cyprus or Cythera. Pan and Aphrodite, both of mysterious birth, both mediating forces (panic, desire, lust, heartache) that were raw and uncontrolled, were understood by the ancients to share a connection, as did Pan and Dionysos, who were characteristically shown attending one another's revels on the vase paintings. The tradition that makes Pan the son of Hermes emphasizes the goat-foot God's capacity for guile and trickery, His manner of appearing when least expected, and perhaps, a hint of Himself as the gateway to deeper Mysteries than many would ever suppose.

A bringer of Light, Beauty, Vision; a gateway to Mysteries; One who guides us and goads us through Terror, Lust, Nightmare, Vision, Ravishment, Despair, Ecstasy, ruthlessly and lovingly into an awareness of unvarnished Truth. Who better to lead the aspirant into the Halls of Initiation?

When I think of Him now, often what comes to mind is a ritual I led in the Summer of 2001 at the Blue Heron Radical Faerie Gathering. Wearing only a long piece of translucent black fabric heavily embroidered in gold thread, I summoned Him forth with a florid invocation, arms sweeping wide, fabric flaring in the late August night air. Faeries assisting kept piling vast desiccated pine branches onto the flames of the central fire, which soared dramatically high with each new offering as the dry green boughs, kindling, released clouds of the most fragrant incense to the surrounding revelers. Drums began to pulse and the dancing began in a long wriggling spiral that twisted in and out, up and down, through the ritual Gate of Death marked by a black banner, and back again through the ritual Gate of Rebirth with its glittering streamers – for Pan has also been known to be a Psychopompos. My new friend Claude, he of the generous smile, long curling locks of sun-bronzed hair, lithe dancing torso and nimble willing fingers, wrapped his arms around my waist and would not let go. We ground and writhed into one another as the drumming quickened and pulses raced. At last we staggered back to my tent as the drumming began to soften and people lay on the ground in groups of two, three, or more to enjoy the night. As we began to make love, even through the haze of my altered senses, I could not help noticing that there was a droning bass-note, a strange blurred music persisting deep through the night and into the pale dawn — as of bees simmering in an amorous adytum of sated sensuality. The Flute of Pan had awakened, calling forth sweet honey for the swarming hives of summer's end — and His Song played on into the first freshness of a new dawn.

Pan's Arrivals: Epiphanies and Invocations in Modern Literature and Lyric

Michael Routery

Like Dionysus, Pan is always arriving. Over and over, he is invoked in poetry and art, called forth from his home in Arcadia to our drained and concrete modern world, as Oscar Wilde put it. Reports of his long ago death (which Plutarch reported as having occurred during the reign of Tiberius) were an error, wishful thinking that was promoted by proponents of a new religion. Pan is coming, but his arrival may be shattering – or liberating. In this essay, rather than survey the vast field of works where Pan appears, I will track the evidence of the epiphanies of some of his invocatory poets and devotees.

Pan was a popular subject in the classical and Hellenistic eras as a casual glance in the Greek Anthology will show. However, in the modern era, literary scholars often write as if poems to Pan are mere conceits, nostalgic or even ironic wistfulness. Yet from the beginning of the romantic era at least, Pan's very presence is clearly being called upon. John Keats penned a "Hymn to Pan" within his *Endymion* (818), calling on the god (in the voice of a chorus) on Mt. Lycean to hear his "humble Paean." Percy Bysshe Shelley in his "Hymn of Pan" speaks for the god:

> From the forests and highlands
> We come, we come;
> From the river-girt islands,
> Where loud waves are dumb,
> Listening to my sweet pipings.

He arrives with a gentleness that toward the end of the poem turns intense as his lust rises. If one doubts Shelley's seriousness in invoking this god of nature, there is his letter from 1821 to Thomas Hogg, where Shelley described a rite he performed for Pan: "Your letter awoke my sleeping devotions, and the same evening I ascended alone the high mountains behind my house, and suspended a garland, and raised a small turf-altar to the mountain walking Pan" (Pennick 213).

In the Victorian era, Pan was a popular presence in poetry, such as the Christian Elizabeth Barret Browning's, disporting himself and eliciting disturbing shivers in readers. Toward the end of the nineteenth century, Oscar Wilde expressed a haunting, aching yearning. In his double villanelle, "Pan," the poet cries out: "O goat-foot God of Arcady!/ This modern world is grey and old,/ And what remains to us of thee?" Wilde describes a London, drab and bereft, a dispirited modern metropolis; then in the second part of the poem he calls Pan back, divining how modernity needs Pan. "Ah, leave the hills of Arcady,/Thy satyrs and their wanton play,/ This modern world hath need of thee."

In contrast, Wilde's acquaintance Arthur Machen, writing in the early 1890s in the fin-de-siecle era of moldering Victorianism, presents Pan as a vision of horror to his London high society characters. In his novella *The Great God Pan*, a brain experiment goes atrociously awry. A young woman who is in a kind of My Fair Lady relationship with her benefactor, an eccentric doctor (Raymond) interested in the occult, after an alteration of her brain, perhaps of the pituitary gland, sees life nakedly in a vision of Pan. The experience leaves her insane – and pregnant.

Another doctor, Matheson, researching this case years later leaves a manuscript which describes his disturbing vision: "The skin, the flesh, and the muscles, and the bones, and the firm structures of the human body that I had thought to be unchangeable, and as permanent as adamant, began to melt and dissolve....here there was some internal force, of which I knew nothing, that caused dissolution and change" (Machen, 83-4). The palpitating, pulsing, decomposing, regenerative essences of life, of zoe, destabilize all of the defined structures that the Victorian world was built upon; this is a vision of the sacred as taboo, as something so frightening, yet full of hidden desire, that it leads some of the characters to suicide.

Another character, Villiers, who is researching the mystery, claims Pan is "an exquisite symbol beneath which men long ago veiled their knowledge of the most awful, most secret forces which lie at the heart of all things; forces before which the souls of men must wither and die and blacken, as their bodies blacken under the electric current"

(79). Dr. Matheson's report of confronting the offspring of the original experiment goes on to note, "I saw the form waver from sex to sex…I saw the body descended to the beasts whence it ascended, and that which was on the heights go down to the depths, even to the abyss of all being" (84). The dissolution of the boundaries between the genders is a rupture so unsettling that it creates a headlong fall into the abyss, a dizzying vertigo. Soon after recording his wrenching vision, Dr Matheson dies of apoplectic seizure.

However, Machen was to express an inner conflict. For though his novella expresses horror, something evil, grounded in a metaphysics where soul and matter are irremediably separate, and in which the god appears at the heart of matter – awe and wonder were at the heart of his own vision of Pan. He wrote, "Here was my greatest failure; I translated awe, at worst awfulness, into evil; again, I say, one dreams in fire and works in clay" (Smith, 8). Yet many sparks fly even today from his decadent tale.

In 1914, as the old order started to crumble in the inferno of world war, Aleister Crowley penned his "Hymn to Pan," which was written as an invocation for a rite in Paris, calling the god from "Sicily and Arcady" in a galloping beat, a strident alliterative call throbbing with a vigor that Crowley's often purple prose did not usually have. "Goat of thy flock, I am gold, I am god,/ Flesh of thy bone, flower to thy rod./ With hoofs of steel I race on the rocks" (Crowley, V-VII). He comes racing, ripping, raping, rending and merges with the 'I' of the poem. In the cracks and fissures of the old order perhaps the god can more easily slip through, as he is called more frequently.

Crowley had already been penetrated by Pan back on December 3, 1909 when he and boyfriend/student Victor Neuburg trekked across Algeria, performing invocations of the Enochian aethyrs in the desert. Near the remote town of Bou Saada they performed a sacramental sexual rite dedicated to Pan, the god shadowing, and possessing Victor (Fuller, 137). Afterward in 1910, Neuburg would also publish a long poem, "The Triumph of Pan." It proclaims the feral joy of that god-ridden rite:

> the lure is mine, and I am fearless,
> Naked, and free, and young;
> The torch is out; no longer night is cheerless

> The hot young day is sprung
> From out the loins of God!
> Rise from the barren sod,
> Raise high the paean of the God in Man!
> In Triumph! Hail to the new-born Pan! (Fuller, 153)

Victor's response is a far cry from Machen's suicidal interlocutors, as the hoof-footed god 'newborn' rushes into the twentieth century. Importantly, the god is now said to be in 'man.' Neuburg's photos from years later show a faunish haunted quality. According to his biographer Jean Overton Fuller, he was never to 'recover' from the experience. Intriguingly, he was later to become something of a mentor to Dylan Thomas.

In the twentieth century, Pan is often glimpsed, if fleetingly, in the work of poets and writers like cummings, Lawrence Ferlinghetti and William S. Burroughs. Burroughs promoted the music of the Master Musicians of Joujouka, whose Moroccan Sufi trance music tradition was rooted in an ancient Berber reality. Bou Jeloud, a goat figure whose dances frenziedly in the festival, was seen by Burroughs and fellow artist and writer Brion Gysin as a local manifestation of Pan. A boy is sewn into a fresh goat skin in the cave above the village, where in primordial time, Bou Jeloud first appeared. According to Gysin, "When he dances alone, his musicians blow a sound like the earth sloughing off its skin. He is the Father of Fear. He is, too, the Father of Flocks…When you shiver like someone just walked over your grave – that's him; that's Pan, the Father of Skins (Re/Search, 48). Fellow Beat poet Harold Norse wrote of his experience of this in his poem, "Pan Pipes of Bou Jeloud." "Adolescent father of skins/ stomping his ancient/ PANIC RITUAL" – the experience brings the poet to "ecstasis" (122-3). In another poem written in 1958 when Norse was living in Naples, "The Secret Pornographic Collection," bronze Pans, exhibited in the special annex of the National Museum of Naples (where the erotic art from Pompeii and Herculaneum is sequestered), the god touches and is touched by visiting young men. "They touch their own genitals/ in sensual recognition/ and soft delight/ as if the church and/ two millennia had never happened" (72). In another poem Norse writes about being in "the hub of the fiery force", in the "red heart of the conflagration" of life, the place where Pan appears.

By the late twentieth century, Pan's arrivals became far-reaching in popular culture and found in many media. Coil's song "Panic" is a particularly evocative one. This British experimental industrial band intentionally produced magical music, often done in particular conjunctions of cosmic forces, with John Balance and Peter Christopherson influenced by the atavistic magic of Austin Osman Spare, as well as by Crowley, William S. Burroughs and other occult visionaries.

For Coil, Pan brings access to important parts of the self that have been shut off, and damaged by the sanitized society of the developed world, the instinctual life many people are so cut off from. Pan is not dead and is summoned in the chaotic beat of their song "Panic." With hypnotic cadences John Balance's voice intones, "Breathe in…put the bone back in," challenging listeners to perform "psychic surgery" on themselves. Perhaps you have felt seized by the state of panic, lost in a forest or hiking on a mountain, where the trails blur with nightfall approaching and the irrational afoot? "We believe that panic is a tool for dismantling conditional defenses," they state on the album cover. A shattering of the ego occurs at least momentarily, where in the liminal zone beyond ego awareness, one senses the little Pans, if fear is not paralyzing. For the ancients there could be many Pans; for Coil too Pan is multiple. "Great Pan is not dead. IO PAN!" The lyrics are haunting and imbued with the terrifying mood that traditionally appears at noon, one I associate with the surge of riptides and undertows, felt in that low bass charge of the music. Coil's lyrics evoke Pan as unsettling, in contrast to Shelley, but unlike in Machen, it is an encounter that can be transformative and mending, putting missing bones back in.

In recent years Pan seems to have a sweeter presence, perhaps god and humanity growing and changing together. For James Broughton, in "Paean to Pan," Pan is the "brashest" of the poet's clan and his "half brother" (73). This is also evidenced in the erotically charged god that queer pagan poet Trebor Healey writes of. His collection is entitled Sweet Son of Pan, and the first poem in the book is "Sestina for Pan," which is labeled an Invocation. The first line begins the quest that leads to a life altering sexual encounter with the god: "Among the footprints I spied the outline of a hoof," the poet becomes field to receive the seed of Pan by the sestina's climax (11). Pan appears in several poems, even addressing terrorism and relating the terrorist compulsion to sexual fear (114). In Healey, there is a re-understanding of the heart of matter, the Dionysian zoe, the over-spilling life, a surrendering ecstatically to that vertiginous falling, that still, however, is far from consensus reality. Not that surprisingly, it seems this embrace most often appears among the works of queer poets.

Pan is always arriving. In the garden of the café where I sit writing his image sits among a flourish of plants, playing his pipes in the cool Pacific air. Can you hear the piping? More and more people are able to beneficially experience Pan's rearranging epiphanies of seething primordial life. At the heart of matter where boundaries of the physical and spiritual no longer make sense, in the mythic domain that lies deeper than the separations of logical thought, in that pulsing, fiery hub, Pan's delirium awaits.

Selected Bibliography

Broughton, James. *Ecstasies*. Mill Valley: Syzigy, 1983.
Coil. "Panic/Tainted Love". London: Wax Trax! 1985.
Crowley, Aleister. *Magick In Theory and Practice*. NY: Dover, 1976 (1929).
Fuller. Jean Overton. *The Magical Dilemma of Victor Neuburg*. Revised ed. Oxford: Mandrake, 1990.
Healey, Trebor. *Sweet Son of Pan*. San Francisco: Suspect Thoughts, 2006.
Keats, John. *Endymion*. John-Keats.com. "http://www.john-keats.com/gedichte/endymion_i.htm"
Machen, Arthur. *The Great God Pan*. London: Creation, 1993 (1894).
Norse, Harold. *Carnivorous Saint*. San Francisco: Gay Sunshine, 1977.
Pennick, Nigel and Prudence Jones. *A History of Pagan Europe*. NY: Barnes and Noble, 1999.
Re/Search. Vol. 4/5. William S. Burroughs, Throbbing Gristle and Brion Gysin. San Francisco: Re/Search, 1982.
Shelley, Percy Bysshe. "Hymn to Pan". Representative Poetry Online. "http://rpo.library.utoronto.ca/poem/1889.html"
Smith, Iain S. "Foreword". *The Great God Pan*. London: Creation, 1993.
Wilde, Oscar. "Pan—Double Villanelle". *The Literature Network*. "http://www.online-literature.com/wilde/2306/"

Panantinous

P. Sufenas Virius Lupus

The ships of Arcadia
go safely across seas
storm-tossed and treacherous
with protection at their prow.

The gods of Arcadia
that protect travelers
like shepherds over sheep
on rustic hillsides.

The sons of Arcadia
in Mantineia's city
who hunt like wolves
in mountainous forests.

The voices of Arcadia
that instill fear
amidst battle's roar,
that shake Hades' gates.

The dancers of Arcadia
wild on the plains
with pipes shrieking
and footsteps like rainfall.

The waters of Arcadia
that drown the careless,
that yield diverse fish
and wash the seashore.

The symbols of Arcadia,
gods and heroes alike,

sons of Hermes,
Pan and Antinous together.

Panantinous, Arcadian god,
protect this ship
and its cargo and crew
from Poseidon's waves.

Bargain

Diotima Sophia

"Tell me now
       what you can offer me
       what bargain do you bring?"

Some service wrought
       And allegiance sworn
       In return for a pretty thing?"

"Not yours alone
       but yours – none the less
       I have promised now to be

I give you love
       I am your priest
       I can give you – only me."

Hymn to Pan II

Rebecca Buchanan

Arcadian Goat

Lord of the Syrinx

Who dances across Mount Lykaion

Who protects shepherds and their flocks

And fills the nets of hunters

    with hare

    and partridge

We honor you

    and your Laughing Sire

    and blue-eyed nymphs

    deep in the earth

Our songs and games

    ceasing only with the dawn

Wild Beauty

Tabitha Few

I would never compare your beauty to that of the rising Sun,
For the Sun may hear the truth in it, and choose to never rise again.

I would never compare your beauty to that of the Moon,
For the Moon is cold and distant
And your warmth could never be frozen.

I would never compare your beauty to the Earth,
Though you are lush and wild.

No, I would never compare you to those jealous three,
For your beauty is all your own.

Clear eyes that see into my soul, hair as fine as silk,
Lips irresistibly soft, a heart as loving as no other.

A special beauty you are, unique, strange, passion in motion,
You are a god beloved by all, a god to whom none can compare.

To Goat-Footed Pan

Amanda Sioux Blake

Goat-footed Pan, I sing
Lusty satyr, son of Hermes
(or sometimes Zeus Himself)
Chaser of women,
Inspirer of panic
Who haunts the wild places of the world
Ithyphallic one,
Lover of Bakkhus's vine,
And of subtle nymphs.
The dancing God
Playing His flute.
God of shepherds,
The bearded one.
Horned God,
Hear my prayer
Expansive spirit of the wilderness
Grant me the freedom
The joy
That fills Your heart.

Thundering Pan

Diana Rajchel

Pan was thundering that night,
Squatted beneath a streetlight.
"Nature always conquers the city,
Come, Witch, stay and see."
The witch sat beside him, Pan-iced with fright.

Four or five cars like lightning went by
Pan dropped his pipes, placed hoof on her thigh.

"I know what you have in mind old goat.
As a merciful human – I'm begging you, don't."
Fearing his horns, she dropped her plea.
"Oh what's the use? Nature can't change for me."

A pickup truck came rolling up the road,
Swaying unsteady beneath its load.
"Look away Witch, I'll save you this pain,"
Pan dropped his pipes into her hand
He liked this priestess, but he was there for the man.

The witch forced her eyes onto Pan's mad dash,
Wincing when at last she heard the crash.
The man in the truck was too broken to scream
The stag hit glass that had run through him, clean.

The witch looked over the bloody and bent hood,
Across the street and into the wood
Pan trickled backwards, melting in rain
Leaving the witch with the man and his pain.
The witch still had Pan's pipes in her hand;
While strangers sought help, she piped songs for the man.

Pan and the Feminist Consciousness

Diotima Sophia

An examination of the ancient texts shows Pan not as a spurned lover, but as a rapist, or would-be rapist who cannot outrun his victims – can a feminist be involved with or interested in Pan? For me, this is an issue which has required thought and adjustment over the course of some years.

Before one can begin any discussion with as exalted a title as this, one must define terms. And, perhaps oddly, the first term in such need of definition is the name of the god himself – or, to put it more clearly, which concept of Pan is to be used in this discussion?

My own preference is for the ancient understandings of the god, rather than the more sedate and indeed all but saccharine (and vanilla) descriptions one tends to find in more modern works. It would be a mammoth undertaking to relate each of these many and varied images to any concept of feminist theory and/or feminism; I trust that I may be forgiven then for concentrating on the ancient (and indeed, far more coherent, for some value of that term) views. "Pan," then, will be defined in this discussion as he appears in the earliest sources, such as the Homeric Hymn.

That's the easy part.

Defining feminism, or the feminist consciousness, hasn't been easy since the word was first used in English at the end of the nineteenth century – and indeed, the general concept has been in dispute for much longer than that. Definitions range from the simple, that women are full human beings with all this entails (Cleage 1993), to the more radical representations of feminism to be found from Daly (1973) to Solanis (Solanis n.d.g) There is no agreement among feminists, particularly among academic feminists, as to what feminism is, and I have no intention of entering the lists by offering any new or honoured definition – hence the title of this chapter is "Pan and the feminist consciousness" rather than "Pan and feminism" per se.

Rather, I shall adopt a middle line between the radical, essentialist views (all women share one burden, all men are equivalent in their oppressive practices) and the stance which focuses almost entirely on obtaining change through legal sanction. As with most people who go through the processes of committing words to paper and the parturition process that is bringing a written work to birth, I firmly believe in the power of language to shape thought and behaviour, but do not subscribe to the universalist idea(l) that all women are oppressed by an inherent patriarchy.[1]

Rather, "the feminist consciousness" here will be understood as a stance for critique, rather than a political platform: one might cogently speak of the lens of feminism as a vehicle through which to view the goat foot god, his mythos, and his story.

Understood in this way, the feminist lens is a concentration of a series of concepts and viewpoints. It searches for and highlights the presence or absence of the female voice, with all of the attendant issues brought about by applying such a lens to what is in the main a body of literature with its origins in oral retellings. It foregrounds the experiences of women (females – in the case of Pan, this would include goddesses, human females and perhaps the odd goat).

Such a lens also takes into account the society at which it is trained: the mythos of the goat foot god arises in a particular time and place. No man is an island and even gods are contextual.

One thing this lens does not do, however, is put Pan in some sort of loco homo – that is, he will not be assumed to stand for all men nor will he be seen as some sort of representative of masculinity. He is, as is apparent through the offerings in this volume alone, rather impossible to box in, and this particular set of boxes fits him no better than any other.

The Greece of Pan, that is, the various states which come under the general heading of "ancient Greece," was for the most part a patriarchal society. This does not mean (merely) that "men were in charge." Literally, it means "rule by the father" and most if not all of these societies were prime examples of what might be called a "proper patriarchy." In general, the eldest male of a family group had almost total power over everyone else in the group: other men as well as women.

Axiomatically, "the glory of an Athenian woman is to be spoken of in neither praise nor blame," which is often taken as a de facto statement of the total lack of voice allotted to women in that society. And, from the point of view of the 21st century, there are any number of practices which rather confirm this: marriage of girls of fifteen to men twice their age, whom they had quite possibly never met, in a ceremony that more or less ritualised rape and abduction; separate spheres of activity for men and women in the home, lack of civil and legal rights, institutionalised slavery and prostitution, not to mention the famous delineation between wives for legitimate offspring, mistresses for bodily needs, and hetaerae (high class prostitutes) for pleasure (Demosthenes). Women were, no matter what their age, always viewed as legal minors in Athens (Gould 1980). Keuls, in a work which is dated but still of interest, waxes eloquent about the significance of the motif of "the killing of the Amazon" as central to the Athenian self-definition (Keuls 1985).[2]

However, we must be clear about our context. As I have argued elsewhere, it seems that the societies of ancient Greece certainly sought to control women, on the grounds that in doing so, they assured the smooth functioning of society as a whole. In other words, the thing about women is (was) not that they were powerless but that, unbridled, they would be too powerful – which is dangerous (Diotima 2004). Women who were out of place (Amazons) or out of control (Agave, when maddened by the god, or Antigone, when she chose to follow the dictates of the gods rather than the state, embodied in her uncle).[3] The reason for this is quite simple: unregulated women are antithetical to a kin-based society which relies on descent through the paternal line. Seen in this light, practices become more coherent and understandable (if in no way excusable).

So what, then, are we to make of Pan in this society, through this feminist lens? The first issue raised by a feminist consciousness might be that of the female voice. Where, in the mythos of Pan, do we hear the words of women?

And immediately we are presented with the paradox that is Echo, whose voice is often heard but whose words are (almost never) her own. Echo could well stand as a symbol of the ancient Greek view of woman: disembodied, placeless, never speaking of her own accord, and giving back only a pale, muted imitation of what is spoken to her. Her very being is one of weakness and reaction rather than strength and purposeful, chosen activity.

And she gets into this state due to the unbridled lust of the goat foot god.

Even a cursory reading of the tales of Echo, Pitys, and Syrinx makes it fairly clear that Pan (in spite of the way he is at times depicted by romantic and indeed, Romantic writers) is no lovelorn suitor, pining due to polite rejection. In blunt terms, he is a frustrated rapist.

This may sound harsh but it does also appear to be the truth.

Pitys, Echo, Syrinx. These nymphs ran from Pan in mortal fear. And, in Pitys' case, to some extent fear of the immortals, as her virginity was vowed to the Athena. While Pan is portrayed as wooing Selene (and even then using deception to attain his goal), it would seem that what he was attempting to use in the case of the nymphs would very accurately be named brute force.

It is interesting to note that the goat foot god, whom we have seen heralded as fleet of foot, swift at the hunt, and so on, seems perpetually unable to catch the nymphs in time. Syrinx stops not because Pan has caught her, but because she has come to the water's edge. Pitys might have been caught eventually, but there is time for her transformation to take place before Pan reaches her. This god who could easily hunt, chase and catch the lynx and hare seems to have been singularly unable to outrun young females – even though he is always seen as a powerful man at or just barely past his prime. I surmise nothing in particular from this, but merely raise it as a point for attention.

That same brute force supervises (in at least one telling of the story) the most horrific encounter with a female in the corpus of ancient tales about Pan. Echo is, for her crime of rejecting the love of men, dismembered as the god looks on, and her "still singing" limbs strewn about the world.

While this is clearly a tale told to explain the origin of the echo phenomenon, it must at least have made sense to those who told and retold the tale – as the functionalists remind us, nothing remains long in a society if it does not fulfill a function for that society. If no one could conceive of Pan being angry enough, or brutal enough, to watch the killing of the nymph, surely the tale would not have survived?

I have called Echo a paradox, and so she is. For while her death (at the behest and under the gaze of Pan) is recorded by one author, in the story of Psyche, Echo is seen "reclining in the arms of Pan." That there is such a contradiction in the lore should not surprise us, but it does serve to demonstrate that Pan is much more than a simple herdsman.

It has to be said that this tale is an unusual one. As we've seen above, Pan is much more likely to be hunting (game or sexual partners) or causing panic and disturbance, than he is to be seen dispensing really quite sensible advice to suicidal young women. The passage seems more linked to images of Pan as a warrior, but one removed from battle; he causes panic from afar, rather than wielding a sword himself. And even in the tales of the death of Echo, he stands and watches, rather than participates directly. It would seem that although he sees a use for violence against humans, to the point of aiding and abetting it, he doesn't himself join in the fray. Again, I draw no particular conclusion from this, merely point it out for the interested reader.

So what is a feminist to make of Pan?

Can a feminist have any sort of relationship with or to the goat foot god, and retain any integrity at all as a feminist? I don't intend to suggest an answer to these questions – they are queries each must answer for herself. But I will suggest two ways forward…

The first is one that I admit at the outset is probably specious, is definitely dubious, and may be simply silly – and which should also carry a caveat as possibly dangerous. It is to suggest that interactions with feminists might have a rehabilitating effect on Pan; that perhaps by hearing, seeing and knowing how the world has changed, the god himself may change.

(But does he need to change? Perhaps to satisfy the dictates of feminism, he need only remember and emulate his interactions with Psyche rather more than any others?)

The second is perhaps more workable and it certainly has more integrity. And that is to admit that not everything in the world is neat, tidy and easily pigeonholed, that not everything surrounding a feminist can accord with her particular philosophy. This is not meant to be a panacea (no pun intended) nor does it remove from the feminist any possible conflict of interest. It is merely an acknowledgement that the world is not as simple or as easy as it might be.

Following this path leads the feminist in weird and wonderful ways; encounters with the goat foot god will test her (or his) integrity and beliefs more often than is comfortable. At seemingly every pass, the feminist who relates to Pan on whatever level must justify what is happening, must examine it, must either fit events into the feminist mindset (however defined) or accept that the world simply does not work that way. Pan is, after all, about being outside limits – and that can as easily include the limits of ideology as it can the limits of propriety.

Notes

[1] It is not surprising, but continues to be depressing, that there is far more agreement among those who disparage feminism, as to what it might be, than those who work to further what they perceive to be its aims.

[2] This is not the place for an in-depth review of gender issues in ancient Greece – this topic has seen lively discussion for a good number of years and information is readily available (McClure; O'Faolain and Martines 1973; Gould 1980; Keuls 1985; Alic 1986; Lefkowitz 1986; Kleinberg 1988; Cohen 1989; Ehernberg 1989; Schaps 1989; Duby and Perrot 1990; Georgoudi 1990; Loraux 1990; Pantel 1990; Rousselle 1990; Scheid 1990; Sissa 1990; Thomas 1990; Zaidman 1990, among many, many others; Duby&Perrot 1992; Katz 1992; Laquer 1992; Lefkowitz and Fant 1992; Bullough 1993; Brock 1994; Maurizio 1995; Beard and Henderson 1997; Thornton 1997; Anderson and Zissner 1999; Metraux 1999; David 2000; Voss 2000; Pratt 2000 ; Larson 2001; Johnstone 2003; Lyons 2003). A fairly superficial review of the essential elements is all that is needed here.

[3] Is it at all significant that Antigone's punishment – living burial – was the same as that allotted to Roman Vestals who were found not to be virgins? The crime, after all, was essentially the same – treason. And the reason for the particular punishment – which killed without bloodshed or violence – the same. Violence against a Vestal was unthinkable, and Creon already had more than enough kin blood to answer for without adding that of a virgin niece.

Hymn to Pan III

Rebecca Buchanan

Goat-footed
Nimble-hooved
God
Who dances sheer mountain cliffs
Twin-horned
Shaggy-haired
God
Who takes delight in deep-watered springs
       chorus of nymphs braiding his beard
              with crocus
              and hyacinth
              and violet
Reed-piper
Hare-hunter
God
Dressed in the pelt of the spotted lynx

Pan

(after Homer)

The Horns of a Dilemma: Beltane and SexGnosis as a "Research Method"

Dr Dave Evans

This is a personal account of some adventures in temporarily becoming the horned God, from the perspective of a magician who is also an academic researcher. The account includes some commentary on the experiences of 'becoming' (possession is not the right word, I much prefer the Haitian Voudun term 'ridden by the Loa') and the academic approach with which such experiences were examined.

Many neopagans in Britain seem to become more publicly noticeable around the end of April for the 'traditional' festival of Beltane, a.k.a. Mayday. In my experience, when attending public group rituals one often finds many more people present at this annual event than any other. This is perhaps because of the element of fertility and fecundity implicit in both the wider world and echoed in neopagan ritual at this time of year, which may encourage many a solitary pagan to feel that this might be the time to meet a prospective new sexual partner after a long winter of solitude, or it may simply be the first comfortable outdoor ritual temperature in these Isles for many to cope with.

In any case, the sexual longing implicit in the aethyrs surrounding such a gathering can be a most useful magical food to employ for ritual activity. Even averagely-done magick is pretty close to the buzz from really good sex in any case, and the 'current' of the symbolic deity-form at this time of year, whether you call it Pan, Herne or something else, can be most invigorating, and enlightening. A week or so before Beltane a few years back I sat down quietly and attempted to 'tune in' to the approaching current, using various meditational aids, and basing this on the rather gorgeous Stag costume which I had made a week previously.[1]

The horned god is thought to represent Cernunnos, a deity similar to the British Herne,[2] or Pan, and it has been adopted by modern pagans as a figurehead for a nature-based religion. This is precisely the kind of animal-man figure often associated with a divinity that appears in numerous historical artefacts, perhaps most notably on the various magical depictions on the Danish Gundestrup Cauldron, a beautiful item unearthed in the late 19th Century and believed to pre-date Christianity by at least a century.[3]

The Horned Helmet and I took part in eight different rituals in that year. Some of these were very public, such as two held in the middle of the internal campsite roads on the site at the Glastonbury Music Festival in Somerset,[4] an event at that time attracting some 140,000 people. Some were performed to large gatherings of pagans at various Beltane events, and in the later autumn of that year the staghead, with me underneath it, presided over a 'handfasting.' This is a neopagan wedding (which, while being intensely meaningful to the participants, has no official status under UK law) for which the horned figure was particularly appropriate – not least because of the wonderful nighttime setting at a large group rite in a clearing in a Welsh forest, lit by flaming torches. Very mediaeval!

This is precisely the kind of terrain in which a real stag would thrive, and we heard actual deer barking earlier in the evening while we were decorating the clearing and generally preparing the site. With wedding ceremonies to some extent being concerned with celebrating fertility, the symbolism of the stag was most apt, and that night was positively charged with a wealth of sexual energy under a beautiful and glowing full moon. The subsequent wedding party was no less wondrous, being attended by some counter-culture celebrities and various hippies, bohemians and free-thinkers.

At two of these ritual occasions I appeared at the edge of the wiccan circle from the undergrowth quickly and 'by surprise,' bellowing like a Stag – this was actually a well-rehearsed and choreographed act done on cue, arranged beforehand with the ritual organiser, but unbeknownst to the vast majority of those present at the ritual. I then recited a series of invocatory, poetic statements that had, as mentioned above, previously been produced 'semi-clairvoyantly' (a minor piece of channelling) and which neatly summed up the magical concept of the ritual being performed. This is the major text (edited for punctuation and spelling from the received version):

> My names are many: Herne, Cernunnos and others
> My name is not important, I am merely a messenger
> The message is Awake! Awake! AWAKE!
> Return to full life within this mortal world!
> Feel the earth awaken, breathe the soft air
> Arise! Arise! ARISE! You children of creation
> For now your land is alive again
> The stars have turned full circle, the wheel is bringing you to springtime once more
>
> You are renewed with the earth, you are open to healing and regeneration, with every opportunity of life before you
> The opportunity to do what thou wilt, and to BE what thou wilt
>
> I carried the ashes from summer's burning, through autumn and through winter's cold
> Those ashes are now the soil to nourish your hopes through spring
> To bring you back to the summer magic, and wonders to behold
> Awake and arise, AWAKE AND ARISE with health, love and happiness, from the spirit of the Greenwood
>
> So mote it be!

During the first two lines of the recitation, and from then onwards, my being was filled with what I can only describe as a hugely powerful divine presence, which "took over" and I was "ridden" by the spirit of Herne (or, based on some of my own previous experiences, this was undoubtedly the God Pan in one of his guises).

The effect was most noticeable to those persons standing closest by, who hearing the power and a 'special nature' with which the words were being stridently delivered compared to my normal speaking voice, were alerted to some magical effect occurring. I finished the recital and stood by, simply shaking inside, while the rest of the ritual was conducted, including the passing round and communal eating of a shared symbolic cake. I ate the cake absent-mindedly since I was attempting to suppress my hysterical laughter within the helmet. The whole experience, while not new to me, had been immensely strong, and quite mindblowing. In the case of the Horned God it is also highly sexual. It proved to be of immense power as an attractant, since had I been of a mind to indulge,[5] several pretty likely (and in one case, positively dripping) new sexual partners approached over the course of the next hour or so, having been hugely impressed by the immense magickal 'charge' which my participation and these words gave to the ritual.

I was unable to hold a 'sensible' conversation with anyone after the ritual for some 90 minutes, during which time I was swept along on a rolling tide of total joy. It was over three hours later that I felt mentally 'safe' to drive my car home. Language is often unable to convey the depths of such religious experiences, but I can find commonality between my feelings then and the written experiences of both Christian Saints and occultists.

Any watching historian or anthropologist who had neither insider knowledge of the topic, nor personal experience of ritual or a successful invocation of any divinity, might have viewed the event in a completely different way. Their commentary might have been brief and damning: to the effect that 'someone in an unrealistic vaguely-resembling-a-stag costume lurched out of the bushes like a clown, read some disjointed poetry very loudly, and laughed a lot... then they all ate cake.'

This is not to criticise the outsider perspective, but merely to say that there is so much more going on internally and subjectively in ritual, which is often hard to historicise from outside. Any observer should also beware of making any moral judgments of the practitioners here – as the sociologist Doug Ezzy points out: "we are not above or beyond the others we study, for the social processes that bind them bind us too."[6] Comparing ritual performance with theatrical performance, as the outsider may often have recourse to do, having no other convenient referent, is often unproductive for the academic; an 'explanatory fiction,' since it merely *describes* one intangible action by using another,[7] while actually explaining nothing.

The sceptical observer at a public event might indeed be tempted to think that this is merely costumed play-acting, however the participants take it all seriously, and 'real' things happen – and even if the play-act element is more overt (for example I have dressed as, and 'become' the heavy rock singer Ozzy Osbourne for a public chaotic magickal rite) the results are still intended to be far more than theatrical… Channelling Ozzy without him being either dead or a deity was pretty damn strange, but that's another story…

I have stated here with some candour (and possibly the risk of academic ridicule) the experience within the Horned Helmet. There is less career risk here than may be assumed, since being currently a freelance researcher I have no actual tenure-track position to risk by being open and honest. However future jobs in academia may be slightly more difficult to find due to my being a 'self-outed' magician.

If Pan has taught me anything it is to be real. Since I would not wish to work for any organisation that did not want to employ anyone on grounds of holding any particular belief the act of self-disclosure is actually saving time in the end.

It is, as the researcher Andy Letcher, himself an academic and magical practitioner, writes: "irrelevant to the scholar whether those narratives refer back to a tangible event or not."[8] What is important is that the narrator re-tells them as if they happened, and then acts accordingly. This is the important angle for historians of magic, since those actions such as my experience with the stag helmet (or their retelling, and belief in them) did happen in a form that can be historicised, while the absolute verification of such things as the presence or influence of non-human entities encountered in rituals cannot, using any current academic tools. Even a brainwave measuring device would only tell us that some very unusual patterns are being created – which I can tell you now, without needing to have them measured – without the cause being discernable simply from the graphs!

From my own perspective as a practitioner I can merely assume that the experiences I have had many times during diverse rituals were the same or similar to those which ritual participants and religious visionaries have experienced over time. As Robert Wallis remarks in his fabulous academic book about Shamanism, "in effect, it doesn't matter how close anthropologists get [to involvement in the subject material] so long as their findings express the level of insight and constructive, critical evaluation that one's academic peers require for outstanding scholarship."[9] As Andy Letcher most valuably points out, our various spiritual experiences are "subjective and cannot be assessed or measured, it forms an invisible currency."[10]

Nevertheless, it is a currency, and if it cannot be counted in a scientific form (or similar) that is meaningful to academics, then it can at least be acknowledged as present. It must also be acknowledged to have value as such, rather than be ignored completely, even if (as Letcher again writes): "within ... alternative spiritualities, there is a predisposition to entertain beliefs about the world which would be considered fanciful by the mainstream."[11] It is the presence of the belief, and the effects on the individual, and on the world they inhabit, of holding that belief, not its likelihood of being accurate, which is concerned in the work of others and myself.

Our task is the recording of the phenomena, and the analysis of those, using various academic angles that can be applied to magic, since academia simply does not have the requisite tools to measure or verify the existence of internal religious experiences as such. It is possible that academic enquiry will never have such tools, and will have to rely on reportage and personal discourse alone.

Many beliefs outside of magic are also fanciful when examined with a scientific rational mind. This would include all religions, for example, and modern physics, where the theory of light requires that light be conceptualised as both a wave and a particle simultaneously, which is both impossible and totally necessary in order for physics to 'work.' This impossible paradox makes some magical beliefs seem almost sane by comparison...

We should also as academics also beware of making any moral judgments of the practitioners; as the sociologist Doug Ezzy points out: "we are not above or beyond the others we study, for the social processes that bind them bind us too."[12] Utterly indispensable advice.

Also in complete agreement with Letcher, I regard being a magician studying the subject as a positive advantage with only a few handicaps, since first-hand experience of magical ritual is vitally important in order to even attempt to understand modern magical practice. I feel that to attempt to study magic without even a slight grounding in the practices and beliefs would be to provide oneself with huge semantic, theoretical and cognitive hurdles.

Pan doesn't care, though, He just *is*, he wants chances to become, chances to ride us and share his joy, and I still feel him burning behind my eyes sometimes.

Notes

[1] This was a snout-shaped helmet, fashioned from a construction-site safety hat and a lot of chicken netting, covered with 'fake fur' (to avoid upsetting vegetarians and to make it lighter to wear) and with a pair of real and hefty stag antlers fitted to the outside. When worn this gave the visual effect of a stag's head being borne aloft a human body. It so happened that this was worn with a forest green-coloured robe, and I carried a large Hazelwood stang, adorned with woven red, black and white ribbons (for blood/egg, semen and soil), adding to the 'nature-woodland' effect.

[2] Herne has a wider cultural place in Britain perhaps due to the 1980s hit TV series Robin of Sherwood, which was widely broadcast (and remains so on satellite channels), and had a large reconstructionist mystical pagan element, with Herne being a regular character as a spiritual mentor to Robin Hood. The ethereal and beautiful soundtrack by the pagan-favourite band Clannad also helped the broader appeal.

[3] The Wikipedia page for this is actually quite good: http://en.wikipedia.org/wiki/Gundestrup_cauldron

[4] This was a syncretic and ad hoc rite which drew on the Voudun notion of the sanctity of crossroads, elements of Wicca, some ceremonial magic, some words from Aleister Crowley, etc,.

[5] At the time I was not; nothing personal to those making themselves available, one of whom was particularly hot. Sorry.

[6] Douglas Ezzy, review of Susan Greenwood, 'Magic, Witchcraft, "Witchcraft" and the Otherworld,' *Pomegranate* 16, p 42

[7] Andy Letcher, Role of the Bard, unpublished PhD thesis, 2001, p 10

[8] Ibid, p 186

[9] Robert Wallis, *The Sociopolitics of Ecstasy*, Introduction, p 4. This is an unpublished PhD Thesis which later became his book Shamans-NeoShamans, London, Routledge, 2000

[10] Letcher, Role of the Bard, p 206, emphasis original

[11] Ibid, p 210

[12] Doug Ezzy, review of Susan Greenwood, 'Magic, Witchcraft, "Witchcraft" and the Otherworld,' *Pomegranate*, 16, p 42

Pan's Mistakes

P. Sufenas Virius Lupus

With Daphnis his love he'd indulge
while the syrinx's skill he'd divulge;
when boy was blinded
by nymph, reminded
was Pan of his passionate bulge.

Hermaphroditos was surprise
to the goat–god's sex–addled eyes,
with breasts of Venus
but the male genus
Pan fled from those exquisite thighs.

With Herakles Pan, mistaken,
panicked, consumed with fear, shaken;
in Omphale's dress
Pan's plans were a mess
when hero's arse wasn't taken.

It seems very petty to gloat
(for one who's not horny like goat)
with Pan—too willing
in lusts' fulfilling—
if love's just known in what I wrote.

From a Distance ....

Diotima Sophia

Janine eased the pack for the hundredth time to a slightly more comfortable position – slightly being the operative word. "Steady on as does it" she repeated the old motto through gritted teeth and concentrated on putting one foot in front of the other. The progression seemed endless....

The fact that she had only herself to blame didn't really help matters very much. After all, she'd insisted that she was perfectly capable of hiking the five miles from the car to camp to meet the rest of them. John had offered – as one would expect – to meet her. But that would have meant he'd walk ten miles in one and day and that she'd have to admit a need for company. The first was a physically doubtful exercise – the second quite simply was not going to happen.

She was a day later than everyone else because of yet another emergency at work. Or, so she had told them. In reality she'd been at the consultant's office – again. Her despondent memory of yet another disappointment carried her for a good hundred yards.

Or perhaps more.... she same back to reality when she stumbled over a tree root that had (she felt) maliciously reached out for her boot.

On recovering her balance, she looked round and realised that she was in unfamiliar territory: clearly, her consideration of the consultant had taken her from the beaten track, and far enough so as to remove any familiar landmarks.

However, even if she were lost, the sun could hardly have moved: the camp was due west of the car park so as long as she kept going in this general direction she was bound to hit it sooner or later.

(She managed to suppress the small voice that told her that if she'd really kept going west, she'd still be on the trail...).

The day's heat was becoming uncomfortably intense, on this early August afternoon. Why was it so now, at two, when noon had been overcast? And *why*, in August, had she chosen to wear such a heavy blouse? It was doing nothing to protect her shoulders from the pack and everything to make her hot and very bothered.

The pack chaffed with every step, and she could feel a blister forming on her left heel. She was over hot, far too tired (the appointment yesterday had robbed her of a night's sleep – again) and becoming more irritable with every step.

"Just as well John didn't come – I'd have probably bitten his head off by now...."

Indulging in the fantasy of a really good argument with the cloyingly protective oldest member of the group, Janine once again lost her footing. This time she didn't just stumble; she fell solidly, and slid, down the steep bank that fell away to the left of her path.

Arriving at the foot of the bank, she lay for a minute, alternating between swearing and taking stock. The swearing relieved her frustration a bit – the stock taking assured her that she'd broken nothing but the strap of her pack. Her pride, however, was severely bruised.

So, she found when she attempted to stand up, was her ankle; enough so that she almost fell again, and grabbed at the bole of a tree for support.

As she stood, fighting the wave of nausea that attends sprained ankles as an acolyte, she realised that for the last few minutes she'd been hearing a small, subtle sound – water burbling over rocks.

Suddenly, nothing seemed more inviting than a stream – and cold water, she reasoned, would be good for the ankle. Leaning heavily on a branch she'd picked up, she followed the sound, hoping the trickle of water would be deep enough to bathe her feet....

"And the rest," she breathed, as she came through the tall shrubs that had blocked her view. Stretching in front of her like and oasis was a calm, and above all, *cool* pond or mini lake, or something....

Not wasting time on definitions, Janine shucked off the pack at the water's edge and sat to remove her boots. A quick glance around assured her of her solitude – the rest of her clothes joined the boots. Abandoning the stick, she hobbled to the water.

The cold hit her as a shock – the water was clean, clear, and above all, icy. In fact, the shock of the cold took precedence over the pain of her ankle, so she was able to walk far enough into the water to lift both feet and float on the surface.

In spite of her previous urgency to join the others – fuelled by the consultant's dire warning that her hiking days were all but behind her

— she luxuriated in the water — resting, revelling in the contrast between the hot sun and the icy water.

Slowly, however, she gained the definite feeling that she was not alone — in spite of all the quite clear evidence to the contrary. Not being comfortable with the idea of being caught skinny dipping in the middle of the day — up and coming young solicitors didn't do that sort of thing — she scanned the trees around the lake for hidden, prying eyes.

And realised the she'd been right — she wasn't alone. There, on the far side of the lake, as if he'd been there the entire time, a man was sitting cross legged and at his ease on a rock. At this distance, and without the aid of the glasses which now adorned the pile of her clothes behind her on the bank, all she could tell was that he was dark haired and wearing dark trousers.

He was also smiling directly at her.

As soon as she'd seen him, Janine had gone from floating face up to treading water. She also knew she was blushing furiously.

If anything, that caused his smile to broaden — he seemed to know her embarrassment and enjoy it; he certainly did nothing alleviate it.

To continue to stare at him wordlessly was intolerable, but there aren't many suitable opening lines in such situation. Eventually, she settled on, "I ... I didn't know you were there."

"But I knew you were here." The smile didn't dim but did become ... quizzical, perhaps? "How did you get here?" He asked.

"I just walked" Janine replied. "I must have wandered off the track a bit...."

"More than a bit."

"I didn't know this lake was here," she added — realising, belatedly, that unlike the path she was used to, this lake might be on private land.

"I'm not surprised you didn't know it was here. It's not, usually."

With that cryptic statement, he turned to go, and almost instinctively, Janine tried to follow. She found that she could reach the bottom of the lake and began to walk toward the bank, till she was reminded of the sprained ankle. The anaesthetic of the cold water had apparently worn off, and she gasped in pain.

The sound, which she'd thought quite quiet, brought the man's head snapping back round to face her, even as he was about to disappear into the foliage.

"You're hurt." It was a statement — and an offer, as he turned and began to come back toward the lake. He looked at her again, lifted his head slightly and said, "You're unwell."

"No, I'm fine, really!" Torn between not wanting to lose sight of him (why, she could not understand till much later) and the knowledge of her underwater state of undress, modesty (or what passes for it) won out and she assured him of her well being. "No, I'm fine, really. Don't let me hold you up."

His eyes held hers for a few moments, but clearly she meant what she said. He finally nodded — and said, "Ok. Sweet dreams." He turned toward the trees, and disappeared among them.

Staring at the patch of foliage which had swallowed him, Janine wondered at the odd thing he'd said. "Goodbye" would have been sensible. "Get off my land" would have been rude but possibly justified. But ... "sweet dreams?"

Collecting both clothes and stick, Janine hobbled over to the far side of the lake; she wanted to see the rock where the man had been sitting. She wasn't entirely surprised to find, behind the rock, a collection of bracken that had clearly been used as a bed. That explained why she'd not seen him earlier — he'd been asleep.

And suddenly, that seemed a remarkably good idea. She felt she could go no further. Cursing the accuracy of the consultant's prediction of increasing weakness, Janine lay down on the surprisingly comfortable greenery.

More tired than she had let herself believe, she fell almost immediately into a deep sleep.... A sleep which included dreams of the man from beside the lake — but now he was beside her — strong arms supporting her. He knew, it seemed, that the sprained ankle was the least of her worries....

And, as always when anyone offered support, she fought him — pushed him away, or tried to.

Suddenly, he was much taller, larger than before, "majestic" was the word that came to her. He was also holding out his hand.

"Think, before you reject it. Remember, *you* found *me*. That's not easy to do. Part of you really wanted, needed, to find me. You know what I can offer — but your part of the bargain is much harder. I give — you must accept."

And then, he smiled.

"After all, what have you got to lose?"

The last part of the dream she could ever remember was her hand, reaching out for his....

A year later, Janine made the trek again — this time in a much better frame of mind, and indeed in much better health. The consultant was confused but very pleased — and she'd agreed to submit to a battery of tests to find out what had caused the unheard of remission.

She knew, now, that there was no lake on the map. She'd checked. She walked on, however, certain that she'd find it again.

As of course she did.

And she found him.

He was again — still? — sitting cross-legged on top of the rock, still clad as before. With her glasses on this time, Janine could see his dark eyes, curling hair, and the softness of the fabric of the trousers.

His smile of greeting held no surprise, nor did hers.

"This place — it's not on any map," she said, as she walked toward him.

"Oh, it is, it's just not here, is all. You found it again, didn't you?"

"Yes, but I don't know how."

"That's easy. Arcadia," he said, "is a state of mind."

She attempted to understand that statement for a minute or two, then shook her head, and asked, "Who are you?"

He grinned at her.

"For a lawyer, you really aren't very observant, are you? Put the clues together, brief," he said, showing a passable use of English slang. "You found me in the woods — in the early afternoon. You were very ill. Now, you are not. The change between ill and well came while you were asleep in my place."

Realisation warred with disbelief on Janine's face and in her mind.

"I suppose you can be forgiven, though," he said, as he unfolded from the rock. "You'd never seen me properly, had you?"

Smiling broadly at the young woman whose eyes now stared in amazement, the goat footed god bowed deeply to her — and was gone.

Hymn to Pan IV

Rebecca Buchanan

I sing of Pan
        curly-horned
Lord of Flocks
        lusty-voiced
Lover of Nymphs
        quick-hooved
Mountain Dancer

Io Pan!

Dithyramb for Pan

Christa A. Bergerson

In Memoriam Richard Hardig Jr.
Timor mortis conturbat me.

Out from the bushes, just below
Look out for the goat clad man

He's waving his phallus to and fro
Pointing to nymphs in the trees

Pan chants:
Your blossoms lure me from the shadows
I must climb down the mountainside now

The nymphs sing sweetly:
We see you dancing 'tween the forests and hills
We hear you laughing with your deep throated shrill
You are the prancing, lusty goat god

Pan chants:
Your hair is glistening, your limbs are sinewy
Must you tempt me with breasts so dewy?

The nymphs sing sweetly:
We hear you playing your pipes of reeds
And serenading birds in the beech
You are the shepherds' wild goat god

Pan chants:
I play for you and the forests and the flock
And every wild thing that crawls after dark

The nymphs sing sweetly:
We hear your cloven hooves tapping
We see your black tongue wagging

You are the ever lusting goat god
Pan chants:
These are my hills and my emerald domain
I forever rule here, it will never change

The nymphs sing sweetly:
We hear you calling from the greenery
We hear you beckoning from the shrubbery
We are frightened of your mighty rod

Pan chants:
Must you constantly whine, will you hide like Pitys in the pine?
Don't fool yourself, you aren't so hard to find

The nymphs sing sweetly:
We see you hop and frolic on jagged rocks
Guarding shepherds and their sleepy flock
Yet you incite such havoc

Pan chants:
Come hither, come hither pretty spirits
I'll take you tonight and spoil your dinner!

The nymphs sing sweetly:
We know the tragedy that befell Syrinx
Your prowess will not make us swoon
We won't be like Ekho - lost to doom

Pan snarls:
I'll take who I want, and I'll do as I please
This is my house and these are my trees!

The nymphs sing sweetly:
Oh sly and impish cock of the forest
Why do you fervently adore us?
You are the potent horned god

Pan chants:
I'm in it for the chase and I'm wild as can be
You needn't be so chaste, no one will ever see

The nymphs sing sweetly:
Oh bewildering Aegorcerus
We plead, don't come near us!
You are the wicked goat god

Pan chants:
Don't resist, I can pleasure you, we would birth such bliss
I promise it won't hurt a bit

The nymphs sing sweetly:
You've got us down on our knees
We're begging you, leave us be
You are the great forest goat god

Pan chants:
When I play my flute, it is meant to soothe
Why must you be such a prude?

The nymphs sing sweetly:
Oh lecherous seducer of the Mistress Moon
Please leave us to our trees
And grant just this one boon

Pan snarls:
Never! I was abandoned by my cruel mother
So now I must take you all for my lovers

The nymphs sing sweetly:
Do you think you tickle us with your fuzzy chin?
That shaggy beard prickles our tender skin
You are the magical goat god

Pan snarls:
Don't play hard to get, to my chagrin
It's purely my right – such a delight to plant Paniskoi within…

God Crush

Jason Ross Inczauskis

She has a god crush.
She hears him as he plays the pipes, calling the nymphs to dance.
She is not a nymph, but she thrills to the music.
She creeps through the woods, to gaze upon the revel.
She watches the Great God Pan, cavorting with Nature's brides.
She gazes upon his horned face with pleasure.
Some may call his form ugly, for it is not entirely like that of man.
She knows better.
Beast does not detract from man, nor man from beast.
Each is instead the compliment of the other.
She sees man and beast together, the best of each, perfect asymmetry.
She sees him as beautiful. Handsome. Desirable.
She watches him move with perfect grace, his dance spontaneous.
It is frenzied, but unhurried. Movement without care, but with pure delight.
It is a dance celebrating the state of being. A physical rhythm honoring life.
It is wild and free, flowing through the god to be born briefly into the world.
She wants to join the dance.
Her body moves of its own accord, swaying to the rhythm even as she hides.
It pulses within her, music in her blood. Drums for a heartbeat.
She dares not join the dance.
She would not presume to be worthy of godly company.
She watches longingly from afar. Desire fills her heart.
It is all she can do to resist. Pan is Desire, but also Fear.
She desires, but she fears. She fears what will come if she joins the dance.
She fears what will become of her when morning comes.
She is afraid. Of her own passions, her own desires.
She fears they will consume her. That there might be nothing left of her.

Another nymph. Another worshipper. Would that be her?
If she joined the dance, would she be his forever?
With the first touch of dawn's light, would she lose herself, all that she was?
Would she belong to him, and cease to be her own?
Would she even mind?
If she lost herself in his dance, his embrace, would she have any regrets?
She doesn't know. She longs to find out.
Her eyes will not leave him. They couldn't if she tried.
She takes in every moment, treasuring it as though it were her last.
She longs to join the dance.
She hopes to see the end of it. Silently, she prays she never does.
She prays that the dance will never end. That she can watch it forever.
The nymphs and their Wild Lord romping together.
A beautiful chase. A hunt where she'd wish to be the quarry.
Each moment more beautiful than the last.
Her resolve falters, and she leans forward the slightest bit.
She wants to be closer.
His eyes meet hers. Panic and desire freeze her in place.
He gives her a lustful, passionate grin, reflecting her own thoughts.
She blushes, her face burning with her own desires.
He continues the dance, his eyes still beckoning to her.
He could make her join, but he shall not do so against her will.
He gives to her a choice.
The invitation has been made, in actions though not in words.
The dance is hers to join if she so wills it.
She steps out into the clearing, standing in the edge of the firelight.
She watches the giggling nymphs and the laughing god.
She doesn't know if she'll join the dance.
She no longer feels like one spying shamefully from the shadows.
She feels welcomed. A part of the revel.
She reaches out to touch him.
She doesn't know if she'll join the dance.
But she had to get closer. She had to touch him, if only once.
What choice did she truly have?
Her fantasies are alive. She could not stop them if she tried.

She shall see him in her dreams, if never again with her eyes.
He is primal passion. He calls to that part of her that is yet untamed.
She doesn't know if she'll join the dance.
She wants to be closer to him. As close as she can be.
She is not his nymph. She is not his worshipper.
She has a god crush.

You Press ....

Diotima Sophia

You press
        Your presence – palpable
How can they not see?

The room resounds
        You presences – looms
How can it be just me?

That sees the signs
        Your presences – leaves
Imposed upon the brain?

You press – and loom
        Your presence – here
Or perhaps – I'm just insane?

But if insanity means
        Your presence – seen
I'll chose it above the mob

I choose not to live without
        Your presence – felt
I choose the goat foot god.

Pan

Michael Routery

O feral son of Hermes,
Rough joy of the traveler,
Bringing bliss to the faces of all gods
On high Olympos among the glittering
Crags. Clad in hare and lynx,
You jump from rock to rock
In the tanglewood
On steep brush-choked slopes—
Where some would but fall to their deaths
— On those splendid feet.

Hymn to Pan V

Rebecca Buchanan

wild-crowned
lord of the hidden song
that echoes
      dances
through untamed lands

mad
mirthful
pan

Io Pan!

Kenn Payne

I sit and wonder beneath the trees,
Waiting for Your whisper upon the breeze.
Deep in my stomach I feel it start,
Working its way up towards my heart.
The leaves all around rustle with no wind,
I hear footfalls in the underbrush –
A snapping twig!?
My eyes dart from side to side,
But the culprit knows well how to hide.
And then I hear it, soft and low,
The sounds of panpipes, from where I do not know.
My heart beats as the panic spreads,
And the wind picks up as though in tune with my dread.
A cry in the woods – a fox or something worse?
I feel my fear rise and cannot help but curse
Under my breath.
I know He is out there watching me,
The sound of his pipes change as if in tune with his glee.
Rustic God of dells and glens, goat-footed one of shepherds and flocks,
Half man, half beast; cloven feet and legs of shaggy locks,
Horns atop your head and a wry look in your eyes as you continue to play.
All falls silent – only the sound of my heart persists,
And between the trees rolls in a dappled mist.
The sounds of the Wild Wood abound all around me,
The swiftness of shadows in the corners of my eyes do I see.
Come to me oh potent god of nature!
Let me see you fully formed before me,
Touch my soul and let me know the very nature of the thing that embodies this panic I feel,
Tangible, hard, raw and real!

By Zeus this is too much to bear,
I feel my despair — I can taste it in the air!
I know you can hear me, you see me, you feel me;
Why won't you make your presence known?
Would it alleviate my sense of fear to know what it is that lingers near?
Or would that revelation be too much for me to hold dear?
My skin prickles and the hairs on my neck stand on end,
My whole body tenses as my mind prepares to comprehend
The feeling of your presence — within and without,
A whisper in my ear that reverberates like a shout!
"I am with thee, more than you know.
"My love for you can only grow, and you shall know me by the feeling in your soul
"I am the one who would devour you whole."
And with that He is gone and my fear subsides,
I have spoken with a God in the place where he resides.
I sit and wonder beneath the trees,
Hearing Your song upon the breeze...

Reports of My Death ....

Diotima Sophia

> "The reports of my death have been greatly exaggerated."
> Mark Twain

Twain wrote this particular quip after having read his own obituary – something which must have come as a bit of a shock to him...

There is, perhaps, a parallel in relation to the Great God, known as Pan. Sometime around the 8th decade of the Common Era, (according to Plutarch), a ship's captain was called by name (Thamus) as his vessel passed the island of Paxos. After his name was called the third time, he was told to announce on his arrival in Italy that "The Great God Pan is dead." On accomplishing this, the captain and passengers heard a sound as of many voices, lamenting the passing of such a God.[1]

Needless to say, some have made much of this, as the death of a particularly Pagan (as in, rural, as well as in Pagan-religious) God, being announced at such a time.[2]

Judging by current Pagan and neo-Pagan practice, however, this announcement of the death of he who was styled "The Great God" was not only premature but was, in fact, just plain wrong. Pan is invoked in the well known "Charge of the God;" his name is used in many rituals, such as that cited by the Farrars as the Rite of the Thirteenth Megalith,[3] as well as in innumerable chants, other rituals, songs, etc., including one (by Incubus Sukkubus) which equates not only Pan and Cernunnos but adds Osiris to the mix for good measure![4]

There is, for some reason, a tendency at the moment to connect Pan, Herne and Cernunnos, almost as aspects of the one deity.[5] I have begun to wonder if this is not another, more subtle, but still erroneous announcement of the death of the Great One. It certainly seems to represent a departure from the way the ancients, at least, viewed the deity.

What is there to connect these deities of Pan, Cernunnos and Herne? While this is not the place to discourse on the attribution of the name "Cernunnos" to the various representations of the Horned God in Europe,[6] the fact is that the attribution is generally made on the basis of the presence of horns/antlers. The same may be true of representations which are labelled as being of Herne.

Pan, on the other hand, is not a deity with antlers at all – rather, he is a ram-horned God. The difference, of course, is that antlers are shed yearly by adult males of the deer species, while horns are permanent fixtures. While the presence (or absence, or growth process) of antlers thus has a significance in terms of the time of the year, the presence of horns means only that the animal in question has attained a particular state of maturity. This difference is often glossed over or indeed not mentioned, in that all of the deities involved are described as "horned", while "antlered" might be a better appellation for Cernunnos at least, and would be more accurate in the significance many Pagans give his story in relation to the wheel of the year – antlers are often grown and shed each year, while horns are permanent features.

Cernunnos, or at least a figure so designated, does have some association with rams' horns. He (or the figure of an antlered man) is often depicted holding, or near, a ram horned snake, which appears to be unique to this figure in Europe.[7,8] Snakes are, of course, traditionally associated with wisdom (and particularly occult – hidden – knowledge, as they live so much of their lives in a manner that is hidden from view); horns, as well, are associated with knowledge and wisdom. Combining the two may have been a particularly strong message of hidden knowledge/wisdom? We can't know, but this seems at least a sensible reading of the iconography.

All of which is very interesting, but leads us no closer to the Great God Pan. What do we know of Pan, from the ancient sources?

First of all, we know that he is ancient. Herodotus (who is reckoned to have died in about 484 BCE) records that the Egyptians listed him as among the most ancient of gods.[9] Pan shows up early in Greek literature, in the Homeric Hymns, and in Pindar. The Greeks knew him as an Arcadian deity – that is, one of the countryside, rather than the city (polis). His association with the countryside is perhaps one reason he is never reckoned among the Olympians: Olympia would have been too organised, too rigid, too civilised for him to be comfortable there.

Yet he is not adverse to those who live in cities, and indeed offered his help to the Athenians before the fabled battle of Marathon, earning himself a shrine from the citizens in return.[10] He had a cult centre dedicated to him in Banyas, (at the bottom of Mt. Hermon in modern Israel), in what was then a thriving cult centre.[11] Whether or not cities were to his taste, clearly he did not despise those who dwelt within them.

Yet he is most at home, and considered most commonly in relation to, the wilderness, the wild places – quintessentially, the places which shepherds frequent in the course of looking after their flocks.

There seem to be three distinct views of Pan, from the ancient sources. The first is the familiar one, the father of the satyrs, the lustful, playful, half-goat figure beloved of the Pan painter of ancient Greece.[12] This is the figure who pursues Syrnix to the edge of the water, where she calls for help from the water nymphs and is transformed through their workings. The play of the wind across the resulting reeds leads Pan to create the pipes with which he is associated.

The second is, perhaps strangely, considering modern views of Pan as linked to Cernunnos and Herne, as advisor. It is Pan who convinces Psyche that doing away with herself will not solve her troubles (and indeed, eventually, after many trials, she is victorious in love).

Finally, of course, Pan inspires the fear (best known at high noon or at the dark of night) of the wild places, the non-rational response to what we might term "that which goes bump in the woods" – PANic. This is an irrational terror. As Pan is linked to Dionysos, perhaps this Panic is also linked to the madness induced by that God in his maenads, when they are driven beyond the bounds of sanity. It is tempting to see in both the Panic inspired by Pan and the madness which resulted from the refusal of the king to recognise the God Dionysus, a sort of reaction to hierarchical authority, "civilised living" and the general rules which surround us – but this is a modern interpretation, rather than an ancient one. The ancient moral is much simpler and clearer: beware what you disturb (else Panic may ensue) and honour the Gods (or suffer the fate of Pentheus).

How, then, do these three views of Pan relate to the idea of the tripartite concept of Cernunnos, Herne and Pan? Or even to the general idea of a "Horned God"?

The answer is that to a great extent, it is impossible to tell. Those who interacted with Pan in the ancient world, at least in the Greek world, left us records of what they did, and why, and what they believed – those who drew pictures and created sculptures of the ubiquitous "Horned Gods" throughout much of Europe, particularly in the lands now denoted as "Celtic" often did no such thing – as we have seen, we only have one instance of the name, for example.

Is it likely that Pan would have been associated with a horned snake, as the Antlered God was? It seems to me unlikely – his wisdom is that of the forest and the lack of rules, regulations and dogma, rather than that of the learned ones.

Pan seems to have been a deity whose prowess continued throughout the year, which is in keeping with being a horned deity, rather than an antlered one; there seems to be no record of belief in a yearly life cycle as is commonly associated with The Horned God of modern Pagan lore.

Conversely, there seems to be little record of Cernunnos as Counsellor, while Pan is clearly seen in this role in relation to Psyche, at least. Nor is Pan's demeanour of lustful playfulness at all akin to the sedate presentations of Cernunnos as a seated, pensive deity.

Are we, in linking Pan and Cernunnos in this way, perhaps presiding again over the announcement of if not the death, then the mutilation of the image of the Great God Pan? Perhaps it is time to sever the artificial link between these deities and look at each for what he is, and what he represents, rather than imposing an uneasy identification between them.

Notes

[1] Plutarch, *Moralia*, V.
[2] Bulfinch, T., *Bulfinch's Mythology*. 1978: Avenel Books.
[3] Farrar and Farrar, *The Witches' Bible*. 1996, Washington: Phoenix Publishing.
[4] *Cernnunos, Ancient Celtic God.* [cited 24.10.03]; Available from:

"http://druidry.org/obod/deities/cernunnos.html"

[5] *To the Horned God.* [cited 24.10.03]; Available from: "http://www.homestead.com/summoningspirit/HornedGods.html"

[6] *The Neolithic Collection.* [cited 24.10.03]; Available from: "http://www.sidhering.com/neolithi.htm"

[7] Green, *Dictionary of Celtic Myth and Legend.* 1992, London: Thames and Hudson Ltd.

[8] *Cernunnos the Stag Lord.* [cited 24.10.03]; Available from: "http://www.lugodoc.demon.co.uk/cernunos.htm"

[9] Herodotus, *The Histories.* Penguin Classics. 1972, London: Penguin Books.

[10] Radice, B., *Who's Who In The Ancient World: A Handbook to the Survivors of the Greek and Roman Classics.* 1971.

[11] *Banyas: Cult Center of the God Pan.* 2003 [cited 24.10.03]; Available from: "http://www.us-israel.org/jsource/Archaeology/banyas.html"

[12] Keuls, *The Reign of the Phallus.* 1985, Berkeley: University of California Press.

The Piper of the Big Wood

Rebecca Buchanan

I

They buried Pa on the first of October, next to the baby girl who was born too soon and died before she could be given a name. The ground was near frozen so the Halvorsons (elder and his three boys) came early in the morning to build up a fire. They spread out the ashes, slowly thawing out the earth. The cattle watched from across the yard, loooing, huddled against the fence. Come mid-afternoon, when Father Pierce and the rest of the mourners arrived, they had the hole dug. The Halvorsons helped Jeremiah carry his Pa out of the cabin, tucked warm and tight into a plain timber casket. Catty had insisted on stuffing her rag doll into the crook of his elbow. She went all white and tight-lipped when Jeremiah tried to remove it and give it back to her. He left the doll, wondering what Saint Peter would think when his Pa showed up at the pearly gates with that bit of yarn and cotton in hand.

The sickness had come on quick. Sunday, coming back from Mass, Pa started to cough. By Tuesday, when Mrs Halvorson brought Doctor Jennings up from Winona, he was feverish and breathing hard, and by Wednesday he was bed-ridden, blankets piled up to his chin. Ma stayed up with him all night, praying and swapping out cold clothes and trying to spoon broth down his throat. Her eyes got glassy with exhaustion and fear. When she finally fell asleep near dawn, huddled in the rocking chair her folks had brought all the way over from England, Jeremiah crept down from his loft. He caught Catty and George peering at him from their bunk. Catty glared at him when he waved for them to go back to sleep (not that they had been sleeping; none of them had). He sat down on the floor by the bed, slowly reaching up to touch Pa's hand; it was too hot, and dry.

"Jer'mih?"

He whispered, trying not wake Ma. "Yeah, Pa?"

"M'box." One hand lifted, pointing vaguely towards the mantle. Jeremiah clambered to his feet, quickly crossing the small living space to pull his father's box down. It was wood bound with copper, the top carved with an odd scene. He vaguely remembered Pa carving it when he was little, right after they came up the Mississippi and settled their plot. He ran his fingers over the relief: a shaggy-legged, horned man with a cow and a goat and a sheep standing beside him, and a great tree rising up behind. Ma had stomped her foot and muttered about the devil and nightmares, but Pa refused to throw the box away. She even dragged Father Pierce out to the homestead; but he was a bookish type who loved the old stories. He spent all that afternoon talking outlandish tales with Pa and little Jeremiah, much to Ma's annoyance.

So the box stayed. Every now and then, Jeremiah would see Pa drop some odd bit of this or that into it. Though tempted — especially after Catty got old enough to talk and started pestering him about it — he never lifted the lid. The box was his Pa's. Whatever treasures it held were for him, not Jeremiah.

"Jer'mah ...."

He hastened back across the room, kneeling down, setting the chest on the blankets. "Right here, Pa. I got your box." Out of the corner of his eye, he saw Catty and George leaning out of their bunk, straining to hear.

"... Op'n't ...."

Jeremiah lifted the lid. The treasures inside ... well, they were one man's treasures. A new, small, nearly-finished wooden flute. A bright red and yellow stone polished smooth by the river. A dried bit of fir and an acorn. Some berries, hardened and wrinkled with age; they might have been last season's blueberries. Part of a bee's nest. A bear's tooth.

"Shoulda tol' you ... years 'go ... good friend, he is ...." A creaky breath. "Saved m'life, saved you, when ... w'first here ...." Another aching breath. A hot, dry hand dropped into the box, heavy fingers feeling around. They closed around the flute, tried to lift it. Jeremiah wrapped his fingers around his father's hand, trying not to squeeze too hard. "Play .... play .... likes m'sic .... good fr'end ...." Another wheeze and another, then a shaky breath, then silence.

A clatter of feet across the floor, as Catty threw herself into the bed and curled against Pa's side. The sound woke Ma. Eyes too bright, she fell against the bed, wrapping her arms around Pa's waist and around Catty. George huddled back into the corner of his bunk, pulling the blankets tight against his chest. He was still there, eyes wide, when Mrs Halvorson came by mid-morning with a fresh kettle of broth and some sandwiches.

Mouth tight with determination, dark hair pulled back in a neat bun, she got them back on their feet. She sent Jeremiah out to the well to pull up water to wash the body. (His legs were numb and his knees hurt. He had to lean on the bed to get up.) She set Catty to stoking up the fire and re-warming the broth, even though the girl had to stand on her toes to reach all the way into the pot. By the time Jeremiah had filled three buckets, Mrs Halvorson had coaxed George out his bunk with half a sandwich. Bundling the younger boy into his coat and boots, she sent them outside to spread hay for the cattle and horses and milk the goats. Jeremiah kept them outside until he was sure that Mrs Halvorson and Ma were done washing the body -- he didn't want to think of his Pa like that yet. Certainly didn't want to see him.

Just shy of noon, Mrs Halvorson came out, stopping on the porch to pull on her bonnet and gloves. She spotted them across the yard, George half-hidden behind an armload of hay. "Jeremiah," she announced as she strode over.

He looked down, digging his heel into the hard earth. "Yes'm."

She stopped in front of him. "Jeremiah, you're the man of the house now."

He dug harder. "Yes'm."

"You know what that means."

"Yes'm."

" .... Good. All right, then. I'll send Billy down to Winona to inform Father Pierce, and pick up a casket from Martin & Myhre's. He should be back in an hour or so. I'll tell him to stay here to help you and your Mother get your Father all settled."

"Yes'm."

"I'll have Mr Halvorson and the boys come back in the morning to help get the plot readied."

"Yes'm."

A pause, then. Jeremiah realized that George was still standing there, still as stone, staring at them over the pile of hay. He waved his hand. "George, the cows're hungry. Make sure that calf gets some."

George blinked slowly, then turned away and stumbled across the paddock.

A gloved hand touched his shoulder. He looked up to see Mrs Halvorson leaning over him, deep blue eyes warm. He was short for his age; or maybe she was just tall for a woman. "My Father died when I was young, too, Jeremiah. I was the eldest of five, all girls. My Father raised me right, and so did yours. It hurts now, but you'll do good." She turned away and strode across the yard. Pulling herself up into the seat of her buckboard, she turned to wave once. Flicking the reins, she disappeared down the track and around the bend and between the trees, creaking and bouncing.

It happened like she said. Billy, all hard muscle and bone, came back in the wagon with a casket. Catty (doll squeezed tight) and George huddled in the rocking chair while Jeremiah and Billy wrestled his Pa into it. Ma watched, fingers laced tight. No sooner were they done then she dashed over, nearly tripping over her skirts, and started poking and primping and rearranging and straightening. Billy tipped his hat and departed, wagon clattering; it was a loud, jarring sound that echoed back through the trees.

All that night, silence. Inside, at least. Outside, the occasional howls and yips of a coyote and the frightened moo of a cow. Now and then, Ma would reach over to straighten some bit of Pa's clothing or smooth down his hair or comb at his beard. Falling in and out of wakefulness, Jeremiah dreamt of rag dolls and flutes and wolves.

And now here he stood, staring down into the ground at the box that held his Pa. What used to be his Pa. His Pa's body.

A throat cleared and a hand touched his shoulder. With a start, he looked up and realized that everyone was staring at him expectantly; or, trying not to stare. Father Pierce offered a quick, reassuring smile and tipped his head towards the casket. Suddenly realizing that they were all waiting for him, Jeremiah bent over quickly and picked up a lump of cold earth. He could feel the cold through his gloves. Quickly, quickly, he dropped it into the hole. It hit the wood with a dull thud. Catty took a step back, bumping into his legs.

"You, too, Catty," he urged her, but she just shook her head, lips tight. He was going to poke at George, too, but the boy's far away gaze made him reconsider. Ma, at least, still had enough presence of mind to follow his lead, though she clutched Mrs Halvorson's hand as the other mourners added to the bit of dirt. It grew into a small pile, thunk, thunk, thunk, thump.

A few at a time, they wandered away; the Crooks and the Simpsons and the Nedders and the Graysons and the Halvorsons (Mrs and elder). Buckboards clattered and carriages rattled and horses grumphed as they rode away. The Halvorson boys pulled out their shovels and poured the earth back into the hole, great shovelfuls, a landslide that buried his Pa. Father Pierce stepped over to offer some words of condolence that Jeremiah didn't really hear, couldn't over the sound of the shovels. He looked up and focused when the priest touched his shoulder. "I'll come by after Mass next Sunday, sit with you all for a while."

Jeremiah nodded, only half understanding.

And then the priest was gone, too, and the Halvorson boys with their shovels, and they were left alone, just the three of them with the fresh mound of earth and the bare cross. Just two sticks twined together. Beside it, a much smaller cross, finely carved with flowers. Pa had made it.

"It's too plain," Jeremiah blurted. He rubbed his sleeve at a bit of dirt on the stick cross beam. "He needs a nicer one."

"Yes, yes he does." Ma's arms closed around him. She wasn't much taller than him. Pa had been a big man. Maybe he would keep growing. "Come spring, he'll have the headstone he deserves." She sniffed. "Now than, sun's going down soon. We need to get the fire back up, and eat, and maybe we'll read a bit, hhmm? Just like before."

A soft mooo from across the yard, followed by some goaty neighs.

"Yes, ma'am. I need to feed the animals first, check on that calf."

She kissed his temple, her nose chilly. "Right, then. Hurry, though. I don't want you staying out in the cold too long." She grabbed Catty and George's hands and pulled them towards the house. Catty kept looking back over her shoulder.

Wiping at the dirt on the cross one more time, pulling his hat down lower around his ears, Jeremiah headed across the yard to the barn and animal pens. The cows were all out of sorts, unused to having so many people and loud carriages around. The two horses didn't seem to care, noses buried in feed sacks. The goats kept shoving at him, trying to get him to drop the whole bucket of feed and vegetable scraps. The half-dozen sheep they had kept for the winter just stayed out of his way, running to the far side of the pen and circling around. Inside the barn, the little calf (a late season birth), was doing better. Pa had insisted on tucking the creature into a stall piled with blankets and hay. Ma had wanted to just slaughter it, rather than waste time and resources on an animal that was probably going to die anyway. Pa had just shaken his head and gone inside to warm up some milk.

He should do that, Jeremiah reminded himself. Get some warm milk. As he bent to rub the calf's ears and nose, something hard poked him in the hip. For a moment, he thought one of the goats had gotten out of their pen and followed him in here, and he turned to chastise the animal. But then he realized that it was something in his pocket.

The flute. The unfinished wooden flute from Pa's treasure box.

Jeremiah pulled it out, squinting at it in the low light. Pa was always making flutes, carving them out of any piece of wood that he could find, then giving them away; once he ran out of immediate neighbors, he started leaving them with Dr Jennings and Father Pierce to give away. Jeremiah headed over to the door, peering at the flute in the remaining sunlight. It was closer to complete than he had realized; just a few of the holes needed to be whittled out some more and the whole thing sanded down and polished. He blew on it experimentally. A loud, irregular squeak. He winced and the calf bleated.

"Sorry," he apologized. He rubbed the animal's ears. "Be back in the morning. Be good till then."

The calf bleated again and dropped its head, watching him as he yanked the heavy door closed.

His hat had slid up his head again. He tugged at it, slowly crossing the yard. In the last little bit of sunlight his Pa's marker and the baby's nearly blended into the trees beyond; just more pieces of wood. He blew on the flute again and got another painful squeak. Through the small window beside the door of the house, he saw shadows against the curtains: Ma with bowls in her hands, George just standing. He pulled out his small knife and poked at the flute, picking at one of the holes to make it a bit bigger. Then another hole. He blew again. It sounded a bit better this time.

Back and forth Jeremiah wandered, pacing between the fence and the grave markers and the trees and the bend in the road. Ma came out once onto the porch, calling him to come in; her breath was a puff of white. He nodded and called back "Yes'm" and paced some more, carving and smoothing, trying to coax music from the flute.

The quarter moon was high up in the cold sky, way up over the trees, when his pacing finally stopped. One high, sweet note, followed by another, then a third. An old song, something Pa had played for him and Catty and George whenever they were sick; Pa had played it for the baby when she died, too. Tilting his head, Jeremiah saw that his steps had finally taken him back to the graves, silvered lumps in the ground. They would be covered in frost come morning.

Jeremiah played. For his Pa and his unnamed baby sister and for himself and Ma and Catty and George. The notes slid and tripped as he tried to remember how Pa's fingers had moved over the holes. Gradually, eyes closed, he found the tune, the notes fluttering, skipping through the darkness. They danced through the yard and over the fence, where a few goats neighed in response, ears pricked. The notes danced and disappeared among the towering trees.

The song came back to him, gliding through the forest, between the trunks and branches. Hearty notes, joyous, free. They came faster. Jeremiah responded, fingers tripping a bit, then finding the pace. The song sped up again, deepened, climbing further down the scale then way back up high again. His blood hummed.

Eyes open now, Jeremiah turned from the graves. He backed up a few steps, sliding around on his heels to peer into the darkness and the woods. A few rows of trees and shrubs along the ground and small patches of frost the sun hadn't touched. He took a few steps forward and the song slowed down, narrowed to a few notes, cheerful, beckoning. A few more steps, brushing passed naked oaks and elms. A few more steps and the song sped back up, climbing higher, merry, exultant. A few more steps, heels crunching, and the house and yard and barn were lost to sight, great green firs and pine and basswood and red oak closing around him.

Jeremiah kept walking. He kept playing. Pine needles softened his steps. His right foot accidentally kicked an acorn out of the way. His lips and fingers were sore. The song skipped around inside his skull. Moonlight stumbled down through the branches overhead, bouncing, casting weird bands of shadow. The song was louder now, closer.

A few steps to his left, around a great-girthed oak, the song winding round and round him.

The Piper sat among the roots of the oak, rough, barky roots that arched up and reached far and then dove down deep. One hoof was casually braced against a bumpy root, the other curled beneath him. Fine goat hair of tawny amber covered his lower legs and thighs and hips. Sprinkles of even finer fur dusted his belly and chest and arms. A shaggy, curly beard of the same tawny amber hid his chin and jaw, growing up the side of his face to a head covered in more curls. Here and there, a spring violet or pansy peeked out from between locks. Two great horns arched and twisted and curled back and around, the right one wreathed with violets and pansies and buttercups.

Bright golden eyes, so brilliant in the night, grinned up at Jeremiah as they played. Jeremiah grinned back, shoulders and torso bobbing in time with the music. He forgot the cold, his blood warm and humming. From the corners of his eyes, he spied other figures; they might have been goats or sheep or rabbits or dogs or bizarre combinations thereof. They danced, too, weaving back and forth between the oaks and pines and elm, laughing, neighing, shrieking. Flowers erupted at Jeremiah's feet, buttercup and daffodil and violet and honeysuckle, and green grass and soft moss. The quilt of bright colors and scents grew, spreading out into the woods as the song grew and strengthened and deepened.

Slowly, oh so so slowly, the song faded, faded. The many sweet notes became fewer and fewer. The field of grass and moss shrank, dried up. The flowers curled in on themselves, petals falling, drifting away. The strange figures melted away, laughter and giggles growing softer, falling away to whispers. The hum and warmth of the song faded, faded, floated away.

Jeremiah blinked, his blood slowly cooling. His head hurt.

The Piper uncurled his shaggy legs. As he rose, Jeremiah took a half step back. The Piper was at least as tall as Mrs Halvorson; much, much taller with his horns. He grinned down at Jeremiah, eyes still bright.

"I thank you for the song and companionship, Son of Paul and Emily."

"You —" His throat felt raw, his tongue swollen. He tried again.

"You knew my Pa."

The Piper inclined his head, tilting it slightly to the side. "We played together often. He was my friend." A quick grin. "Still is. I hope we may be friends, too, Jeremiah."

"Are you the devil?" The question blurted out before he could stop it.

The Piper's eyes crinkled and his head fell back. Great gusts of laughter exploded from his chest, wild and jolly and wise. The trees shook and dried leaves fell around them. Jeremiah thought he heard answering laughter and howls from the darkness. When the Piper could finally contain his mirth, he answered, gasping. "Older, I am, than your fallen angel. And no friend of his." He stepped around Jeremiah, fairly skipping, hooves light. "But a friend of yours, oh yes." The Piper edged passed a sapling oak; at his brief touch, buds sprouted, leaved, greened, unfurled -- only to brown and dry up and fall as he disappeared deeper into the forest. The Piper's voice rolled back to him, weaving among the trees. "A gift of thanks for your song. Look for her, at dawn."

II

Jeremiah awoke to Catty poking him in the ribs. He blinked. She poked him again, harder.

"Ow," he muttered and batted her hand away. "What? What's matter?" He blinked again. Pale grayish light turned the curtains from a robin's egg color to something more like periwinkle. Early, than. Very early.

"I hear something. Ma's still 'sleep."

He wrinkled his nose and propped himself up on his elbows. He was back in his loft. He vaguely recalled trudging home through the woods, finding his way by memory and smell and sound. Putting the flute back in the box on the mantle. Ma had given him an odd, annoyed look and shoved a bowl of hot stew in front of him. And ... he must have fallen into bed after that.

Catty poked him again, holding onto the top of the ladder with her other hand. "I hear something. Ma's sleeping and George is too little and too chicken to go look."

"Hear something where —"

A faint scrabbling of claws, a soft tread on the front porch. Jeremiah peered down, but couldn't see anything through the curtain. He pushed the blanket aside. "Look out, Catgirl." She slipped down the ladder, moving aside a half step to let him pass.

George was huddled in their bunk, blankets pulled tight around his shoulders. His eyes were big.

"See, too chicken."

Jeremiah poked aside the curtain. "Shush, Catty — aah!" A furry grayish-black face leapt towards the window and a great pink tongue slobbered all over the glass.

"What's all the noise?" Eyes puffy, hair covered by a cap, Ma peered at them from her bed. She looked small, alone, beneath the covers.

"Sorry, Ma." Jeremiah pulled on his boots, stacked neatly next to the door. "I think there's a dog outside. Maybe one of the neighbor's...."

He cracked the door open. Wider. There the dog sat, tongue dangling, ears perked, tail thump-thump-thumping. Amber eyes glinted up at him, grinning. A loud rhwoof had George pulling the blankets over his head, followed by another rhwoof.

Jeremiah stepped out onto the porch, breath misting, Catty so close behind that she bumped into his legs. The dog tilted its head, one ear flopping over.

Catty knelt down and held out her hand. "Puppy."

The animal dipped its head to sniff at her palm.

"Careful, Catty, it could bite."

The dog's head popped up at that. The animal seemed to glare at him in affront. Jeremiah took a surprised step back, running into Ma.

"Well." Heavy shawl clasped tight at her throat, she squeezed around him. "I don't recognize it. But, I suppose it coulda come from the Halvorsons or the Crooks."

"Not an it," Catty corrected, stroking the dog's nose. "She."

The dog's tail thumped some more.

Jeremiah slowly turned his head and squinted at the woods, eyes narrowed against the brightening light.

"She needs a name," Catty announced.

"Catherine Teresa, we are not keeping that animal," Ma responded severely.

"But —"

"I don't know, Ma," Jeremiah interrupted, eyes still on the woods. "Might be good to have her around for the winter. Chase off the rodents and the foxes and such."

Ma hrrumphed. "Mmmm. I suppose." She hitched her shawl closer. "But it'll have to earn it's keep around here, just like everyone else." She turned on her heels. "Come on, back inside. It's too cold to be out without your breakfast."

Catty leapt to her feet. "Come on, doggy."

"*Not* the dog —"

The dog had other ideas. Ruffing happily, she shoved passed Ma, following Catty inside. She sniffed at the floor, tail high. Sniffed at the air. Sniffed around the room, passed the small table and the cupboards and the fireplace with the longrifle above and the big bed and the rocking chair, finally stopping in front of George and Catty's bunk. The dog plunked her head down on the edge of the bed. George stared at the dog from beneath the blankets. Catty scrambled up beside him.

"What about Princess?" she suggested. "Or Duchess? Or Princess Duchess? Or Presidentess?"

Ma threw up her hands in resignation and strode over to the fireplace. "There's no such thing as a Presidentess, Catherine Teresa." She pulled out the kettle of last night's stew, left to simmer over the coals.

"Well, there could be …."

Shaking his head, trying not to smile, Jeremiah pulled on his coat and gloves and hat. "Be back in a few minutes."

"Presidentess. Presidentess Henrietta. Presidentess Henrietta Anna …."

The smile he had been trying to suppress turned into laughter as Jeremiah closed the front door. The ground crunched beneath his boots as he crossed the yard. The cows mooed and the goats neighed in anticipation. His steps slowed, briefly stopped, as the two crosses caught the corner of his eye. The sun was just up, gilding the finer carvings of the baby's marker and the plain wooden sticks of Pa's grave. His laughter fell away. His eyes slowly rose from the grave markers and focused on the woods beyond. Ordinary looking trees. Just the same elms and pines and basswood that grew everywhere around here.

Tugging his hat lower down around his ears, Jeremiah set about caring for the animals. By the time he was done throwing hay around, tossing out vegetable scraps and dried apples, shoveling out the worst of the muck and manure, disentangling a stupid sheep from the fence, and bottle-feeding the little calf, he was sore and very very hungry. Inside, he found the fire going and George and Catty at the table, a couple of books and a small chalk writing board spread out in front of them. The dog lounged at George's feet, the boy's stockinged toes buried in her belly. Every now and then, he bent down to rub her ears.

The dog, Catty informed him, was to be addressed as Presidentess Henrietta Anna Paulina Thomasina Medley.

Ma rolled her eyes.

The name lasted three days. By the time Mrs Halvorson arrived early Friday to help dye their clothing black and collect some of Pa's things for the poor box, the name had degenerated to Henri. English pronunciation, not French. Mrs Halvorson and Henri inspected one another for a few tense moments, heads tilted.

"Looks like a useful animal," the Mrs finally granted, and the dog barked. "Mr. Franklin's almanac predicts a cold, long winter. We'll have foxes to worry about. Maybe even bears and wolves."

Henri's ears flattened.

III

Just as Mr Franklin had predicted, winter came hard and cold and fast. Father Pierce rode up the Sunday after the funeral, and spent the afternoon reading the Psalms and coaxing a giggle out of Catty by pulling coins from Henri's ears. But he was their last visitor. The frosts of early October gave way in a night to a sleet that turned to tacky, concrete-hard ice. Trees splintered with loud bangs, sending birds to panicked flight. The muddy ruts in the yard became craggy, icy traps for feet and hooves and wheels. The few cows who ventured out of the barn slipped and slid around the pen; the goats laughed; the horses ignored them. Fearing broken legs, Jeremiah coaxed and dragged them back inside. The sheep, surprisingly, proved smarter, only sticking out their noses before retreating to the back of the barn.

Pa's grave marker cracked clean through and George spent the better part of that first morning trying to find just the right sticks to make a new one. Henri dutifully followed the little boy around, carrying sticks in her mouth or dragging branches too big for George. After watching anxiously from the window for a time, Ma finally came out, picked two sticks, took George firmly by the hand, and led him back into the house.

They didn't make it back down to Saint Michael's for Mass again until the Sunday before Christmas Eve. A slight warming had melted the ice just enough to soften the roads and let their wagon through; it was a bumpy drive that took them twice as long as usual. Ma was insistent that they attend, though. "I won't have folks gossiping that we're not good Catholics, or that I've taken to my bed with grief and I'm neglecting my children. Stop making faces, George. You need to be buttoned up all the way or you'll catch your cold."

It was after Mass, as he warmed his hands around a mug of coffee and kept a close eye on Catty (busy stalking the Halvorson's youngest), that Jeremiah heard about the wolves.

"They hit the Tidwells," big Billy Halvorson was telling a group of men, face serious. "You know them, Jeremiah? The Tidwells?"

"...Um, no." Jeremiah shook his head, confused that he was being included in an adult conversation. Man of the house now. Straightening his shoulders, he edged closer.

"Just north of Rollingstone," Billy was explaining. "Lost three in one night. Two cows and an old bull."

"Ey." One of the men shook his head, sipped his coffee. "Too cold. They're hungry."

Another man scratched at his beard. "They'll stick to the bluffs and the woods. Easier for 'em to hide."

Billy again. "Mr. Crook is certain he heard them last night."

"Ehf." Sip. "They couldna gotten this far in only a couple of days."

Catty pounced and the youngest Halvorson shrieked. Jeremiah hastily excused himself.

Ma frowned and tucked the blanket tighter around George and Catty when he told her about the wolves. The wagon hit a deep rut and she had to grab her hat. Jeremiah grunted and the horses huffed and strained and pulled the wheels over the lip of the rut. "Your Pa always admired those beasts. Never understand why, since you and he were almost killed by them."

Catty's head popped around. "Jeremiah almost got eaten by a wolf?"

Ma's mouth tightened. She grabbed her hat again as they rolled up and down and over another rut.

grunt "Pa – um – I heard something ...."

Ma glowered at him. "What did you hear? Who told you something?"

"Uh, well, nothing specific." Jeremiah concentrated on the road, leading the horses around a rut that had turned into a half-frozen crater. "Just that something happened right after we came up the river, right after we settled the farm." He darted a glance to the side. George and Catty's heads were swiveling back and forth between them, necks craned up.

Ma's eyes were dark with disapproval. "Mmph," she finally huffed. "Your Pa got it into his head to go blackberry picking. Foolish notion. And took you along, you, not even old enough to tie your shoes. But he wanted blackberries, so off he marched, you up on his shoulders. Big basket. When you weren't back by sundown I started to worry." A rough shake of her head. "It was well after dark by the time you two came back. Your Pa's clothes were all torn and – there was blood on his clothes. He said a pack of wolves came after you." She shifted in her seat, rolled her shoulders, like she was trying to shake off the bad memory. "You were sound asleep in your Pa's arms when you came home that night, but you had bad dreams for weeks after. Goatmen." She hmmphed. "That's part of the reason why I was so mad at your Pa when he made that treasure box of his – you remember. I was afraid it would bring your bad dreams back." She waved her hand dismissively, then twisted around to tuck the blanket tighter under George's chin. "But, they never did."

IV

That evening, Henri heard the wolves first. She lay beneath the table, George's toes curled into her back as they ate dinner: hot beef and vegetable stew and thick bread with cheese and big mugs of milk. Catty was regaling them with her version of The Flood, in which the silly sheep got lost en route to the Ark, when Henri suddenly lifted her head. Her ears perked then flattened against her skull and a low growl rumbled around the room. The dog slowly lifted to her feet, steps smooth and silent as she moved towards the door.

"What's wrong with Henri?" Catty whispered, eyes big.

A low, low howl. An answering howl. Frightened, high-pitched moos and neighs.

Jeremiah rose to his feet and stepped over the bench. When he lifted the longrifle down from over the fireplace, Ma pulled George closer. Jeremiah padded over to the window, poking aside the curtain with one finger. Henri growled again, making the hair on his arms stand on end. He squinted, trying to see in the sliver of moonlight.

Another howl, closer this time, and longer.

He cracked open the door and started to slide through.

"Jeremiah ...!" Ma hissed.

"Stay here," he whispered back.

"Your coat!" she snapped.

Scowling slightly, half out the door, Jeremiah grabbed his coat off the hook and awkwardly pulled it on, passing the rifle from one hand to the other. He staggered as Henri pushed between his legs, belly low to the ground.

"Stay here," he whispered again and closed the door. He winced at the squeak and rasp of wood, and turned to find that Henri was already half across the yard. The dog's ears were perked, her tail stiff. He could hear the cows dancing around inside the barn, the sheep and goats neighing and bleating to one another. He stopped on the edge of the porch, breath great white puffs. His lungs were already beginning to hurt. He squinted harder, peering around the yard, down the road, along the edge of the woods —

— something dark, a streak, darted across the road towards the barn. A second streak followed. A loud howl, very close, just inside the woods. Another howl, this one from behind the house.

They were encircling the farm.

Jeremiah stopped breathing.

Hungry. And *smart*.

Henri's growl vibrated along his skin. He shivered and hefted the rifle, setting it against his shoulder. "Henri," he whispered, "get to the barn." Jeremiah stepped off the porch and immediately staggered, heels slipping on the icy ground. He caught himself on the support post, nearly losing his grip on the rifle. Righting himself, momentarily wishing Pa had been one of those men to teach his son proper swearing, Jeremiah followed the dog more gingerly. Ice-hardened mud crackled under his steps. His breath came in fast, white puffs.

A loud, commanding howl from the edge of the woods.

Jeremiah spun on his heel, slipping, staggering, righting himself, leveling the rifle.

Another howl, answering from the far side of the barn. Then a third, behind him, somewhere between the barn and the house.

Henri growled in answer. The sound started low in her throat, rose, rose, louder. Goose bumps ran up and down Jeremiah's arms and legs as the growl grew louder, more ominous, threatening. The howls abruptly cut off. Henri's growl turned to barks and snarls, blood-chilling, terrifying, echoing up out of her chest and through the icy dark.

An arrhooo from the woods. More snarls from Henri. The arrhooo died away and something moved. Jeremiah squinted hard, peering down the barrel of the rifle. A largish shape, furred, separated from the darkness of the woods. It stopped just to the left of the graves, eyes bright. A wolf, a large wolf, much too skinny for its size but still powerful. Lips curled back and teeth gleamed as brightly as its eyes. It lowered its head.

A faint crunch and whoof behind him. Jeremiah spun, falling, rifle slipping. Another wolf, mostly brown, some black, charging straight at him. The rifle went off. He didn't remember pulling the trigger, just felt the breath-stopping kick against his chest. A shrieking whine. Burning powder in his nose. Pounding, ringing in his ears. Icy mud dug into the back of his legs and his bottom. Henri was gone. Sounds of panic in the barn, wild neighs and frantic loos and hooves kicking against wood.

Jeremiah scrambled to his feet, took a few running steps towards the barn, fell, banged his knee, got up again, kept running. He shoved open the barn door; the track and wheels squealed. Cows wild with fear thundered past him, banging into the half open door, shoving it open the rest of the way. He had to twist out of the way, wait for the panicked herd to pass. He pushed into the barn past a few straggling goats and sheep, holding the longrifle like a club now, blinking in the dusty darkness. A weak, frightened bleat. The calf.

Wolf. He caught a momentary glimpse of it as it dashed out of the calf's stall, across a narrow slice of moonlight, and straight at him. Teeth. One step back, a hard swing. A loud crack and a thud and a whine and the vibrations ran up the barrel into his arms and shoulders. The wolf slammed into a post, staggered, coughed blood, and collapsed. The calf was still huffling and mooing in terror.

A quick circuit of the nearly-empty barn. A few goats and sheep here and there, and the two horses in their stalls. One of the sheep was dead and one of the older cows, though in the dark he couldn't be sure if the wolf had gotten them or they had been trampled.

Check the calf. It was up on trembling legs, eyes wide. He threw a blanket over it with one hand and dashed back out into the open yard. A couple of cows and a bull were staggering around, and the rest of the sheep were pressed up against the side of the barn. No sign of the rest of the cows or any of the goats.

Loud snarls and yelps from the graves. Henri. He tried to run, but the ground was too uneven. He tripped and stumbled and finally got close enough to see. Henri was atop the alpha wolf, its throat between her jaws. One of her ears was half-ripped off and there was a deep gash across her left hip. The wolf's legs were twitching and kicking. Three other wolves stood near, backs arched in submission. They whimpered and whined, backing away. Henri snarled again. There was a crack and the alpha went limp. The three remaining wolves turned and dashed into the woods, disappearing amid the trees. They howled as they ran.

Henri released the dead alpha and its head smacked into the frozen ground. She looked up at him, eyes filled with a strange sadness, blood around her muzzle. She tried to walk over to him, but fell.

Jeremiah started shouting then, and Ma came running out of the house. She had her cloak on, but not her hat or gloves. Catty and George followed a moment later, though she yelled at them to get back inside. Catty stopped short when she saw the wolf he had shot, and stared. He handed the rifle to Ma, rambling about how he had shot one and hit one in the barn, but the calf was okay, and Henri had killed one with her bare teeth. He wrapped Henri up in his coat and lifted her into his arms, staggering under the dog's weight, nearly tripping again when George ran into him and grabbed Henri's paw.

He refused to get out of the way as they slowly made their way across the yard.

They made up a pile of blankets in front of the fireplace, and cleaned out her wounds with alcohol and washed the blood from her muzzle. Henri laid there for the next week. Jeremiah pulled the flute out of his Pa's treasure box and played that old tune for her, the same his Pa had played for him when he was sick, the same he had played that night when he met the Piper. George often slept curled up next to her. Ma fed her fresh, chopped meat with bread soaked in milk. Catty told her nonsensical stories about rabbits that lived in the Garden of Eden; every time Catty said the word "bunny" Henri's tail would thump. Mr Crook, who had some experience with sick and injured dogs, came over and checked her wounds and peered into her mouth and her ears.

"Yep, yep," he nodded. "Looks to be healing good. Better than I woulda expected. Tough dog ya got here."

By the end of the week, Henri was running around the yard again, corralling skittish sheep into the barn. A few had wandered back on their own, while the rest were returned by neighbors who found them in their own pastures or while out hunting. One afternoon, Mrs and elder Halvorson came up the road, driving all the goats ("Found 'em by the duck pond.").

Word spread quickly of the wolf attack and Jeremiah found himself cornered after Mass more than once by folks who wanted to hear the tale. There were hearty thumps to his back and handshakes. He overheard Catty relating the story to Billy Halvorson, who nodded and didn't appear the least astonished that Jeremiah and Henri had fought off two dozen wolves the size of Clydesdales with only their bare teeth and a rifle for a club.

In the years that followed, Henri whelped three litters of five, six and four pups. Jeremiah was never sure as to the sire of said pups, as Henri never seemed to venture away from the farm. Ma speculated that it was one of the Crooks' sheep dogs. The pups all proved to be just as smart and loyal and brave as their mother and were in high demand among the neighbors. They traded one to the Nedders for a season's worth of cheese, and two others to the Simpsons for a prime bull. Other pups and later grandpups they sold, bringing in enough money to add proper bedrooms and a second floor to the house. The middle pup from the first litter, with one black ear and one white, bonded with George on sight. And, when George was of age, the two paid their respects to the graves by the edge of the woods and then set out West together. Occasionally, a letter found its way back and Ma would stop whatever she was doing to read it, and then read it again.

A few months after his wife died in childbed and left him with three little ones, Billy Halvorson came to the house, hat in hand, and asked permission to court Catty. Catty smiled, Jeremiah sighed, and Ma said yes. They were wed just after midsummer and, along with her hope chest, she took along two of Henri's grandpuppies. They quickly proved their worth, saving Catty's youngest stepdaughter from a nest of rattlesnakes.

As for Jeremiah, like many other young men, he went off to save the Union. He returned with a bullet fragment in his right leg and a limp, and found that the Crooks had sold their farmstead to an Irish family. Ma muttered that at least they were Catholic. Jeremiah met Aisling O'Brien when she came down the road with an armload of rhubarb; a bribe in exchange for some butter, she explained, blowing red curls out of her eyes. Henri barked, tail thumping when Aisling bent down to scratch the dog's ears. The rhubarb spilled out of her arms and all over the muddy ground. Jeremiah gave her the butter anyway.

When Ma realized that his leg didn't hurt as much when Aisling was around, she threw up her hands in grudging consent. The grudging consent changed to warm acceptance when her first (perfect, absolutely perfect) grandson was born ten months later. They named him Paul Patrick, after his grandfathers.

And one morning, when Paul Patrick had just turned three, Jeremiah awoke to find Henri laying by the door surrounded by a passel of her remaining grown pups and half-grown grandpups. They all looked at him with big eyes, not making a sound. For a moment he didn't breath. But then Henri slid her head around to look at him, a head long gone gray and white, and he knew it was time.

Lifting herself slowly, Henri followed him out into the garden, where he found Aisling and Ma and little Paul Patrick. The boy was helpfully pulling up pepper and pea and rhubarb seedlings they had just planted.

"Here now, boy, what do you say we get out of the ladies' way, hmm?" His son poked at Henri's nose then grinned up at him, head tilted back, eyes brighter than the sky. "That all right with you two?"

Ma grunted, hands filled with limp pepper plants.

"Of course." Aisling smiled and planted a soft kiss on his cheek, and then Paul Patrick's. She gently rubbed Henri's ears. "Where are you off to?"

Jeremiah took his son's hand. "We're going to pick blackberries."

From Arcadia With Love: Pan and the Cult of Antinous

P. Sufenas Virius Lupus

Few deities in Greek religious culture are tied as closely to the ancient region of Arcadia as is Pan.[1] Arcadia — both in ancient times and as a modern prefecture in Greece — occupied the central part of the Peleponnese, which included Mt. Lykaion, a famous site associated with both Zeus and werewolves, often through the figure of Lykaon.[2] The Arcadians were considered a particularly ancient population, said to be older than the moon (*proselenoi*),[3] and indeed the language spoken there retained many archaic features well into the classical period of Greek history.[4] There was also a phrase commonly used in ancient Greece, that "to honor Pan" was to engage in male homoerotic activity.[5] Indeed, this image of Greek homoeroticism and its connection to Arcadia persists even to modern periods, and was particularly common during the Romantic periods of the 1800s and into the early twentieth century.[6] The character of Pan, therefore, evokes a timeless and ancient, perhaps even primal, period in Greek culture, and his cultus and associations continued to have a character that straddled the boundaries between rural and civil, chaotic and tamed, domestic and wild.

A prominent city of ancient Arcadia was Mantineia, one of the few Greek cities whose main purported founder was a woman, Antinoë. The heroine Antinoë, as reported by Pausanias (8.8.4-5), followed a snake (or a dragon) in order to select the spot at which to build her city after Mantineus, a son of Lykaon, had founded the original city named after himself.[7] A hero-shrine was located in Mantineia for Antinoë, which was also the public hearth (*Hestia koine*) of the polis.[8] Among the other temples and hero-shrines in Mantineia was the grave of Arkas, the namesake of the Arcadians, as well as temples to Asklepios, Leto with Apollon and Artemis, Zeus, the Dioskouroi, Hera, Aphrodite, and Athena.[9] And, when Pausanias lived, he also reports that the newest temple in the city was that of Antinous.

"He was a great favorite of the Emperor Hadrian. I never saw him in the flesh, but I have seen images and pictures of him. He has honors in other places also, and on the Nile is an Egyptian city named after Antinous. He has won worship in Mantineia for the following reason. Antinous was by birth from Bithynium beyond the river Sangarius, and the Bithynians are by descent Arcadians of Mantineia. For this reason the Emperor established his worship in Mantineia also; mystic rites are celebrated in his honor each year, and games every four years. There is a building in the gymnasium of Mantineia containing statues of Antinous, and remarkable for the stones with which it is adorned, and especially so for its pictures. Most of them are portraits of Antinous, who is made to look just like Dionysus."[10]

We also learn that the Emperor Hadrian had a special connection to the site of Mantineia beyond this, for during the late 3rd century BCE, the city changed its name to Antigoneia in honor of Antigonus of Macedonia, but the emperor Hadrian restored its original name during his principate,[11] and he also restored the sanctuary of Poseidon Hippios just outside the city.[12] Further, the games in honor of Antinous took place on a race-course outside the walls of the city.[13] In an inscription by C. Iulius Eurykles in Mantineia, Antinous is honored as "the local god" (*epichorios theos*).[14] These matters alone – his ethnic origins, his honoring in Mantineia, and even his name (Antinous is the masculine form of Antinoë) – associate Antinous heavily with Arcadia.[15] And yet, there are further associations between Antinous and Arcadia, and between Antinous and Pan, which is the subject of the discussion to follow in the present essay.

One of the most interesting connections between Antinous and Pan concerns a popular tradition relating to the birth of Pan from Penelope, the wife of Odysseus, and Pan's paternity in that story being from Hermes. Hermes has many connections to Antinous, and he is called Neos Hermes[16] or "the god Hermes under Hadrian"[17] on a number of occasions, the "son of the Argos-slayer" (i.e. Hermes) in a poem fragment from Oxyrhynchus,[18] and he is elsewhere given Hermetic epithets (e.g. at Delphi, where he is called Heros Propylaios).[19] A line from the epitome of pseudo-Apollodorus'

Bibliotheke states the following: "But some say that Penelope was seduced by Antinous and sent away by [Odysseus] to her father Icarius, and that when she came to Mantineia in Arcadia she bore Pan to Hermes."[20] For the variety of reasons which this passage is intriguing in terms of what it tells us about Pan, Hermes, and Penelope, it is also noteworthy that the only other "Antinous" of major note in classical literature and history – the principal suitor of Penelope in Homer's Odyssey – is here said to be the cause of her being sent away to Arcadia in the first place. The connection of this birth of Pan via Hermes through Penelope (and, to an extent, because of the suitor Antinous) at the specific location of Mantineia, further, makes the connections between Pan and Antinous the Bithynian boy all the larger.

In the poem from Oxyrhynchus that names Antinous as "son of the Argos-slayer," there are further Arcadian allusions that tie in to the narrative of Pan's Arcadian birth by Penelope, and also Arcadia generally. Argos, as well as being a many-eyed monster that Hermes slew, is also the name of Odysseus' faithful dog, with whom he has a short reunion before coming to reclaim Penelope at the end of the *Odyssey*.[21] Greek poets in the Hellenistic and Late Antique periods loved to allude to Homer in their works, and perhaps an interesting Homeric "contrast" is being established here between the "son of the Argos-slayer" (Antinous the Bithynian) and, therefore, Argos – but not the monster Argos, rather instead the canine Argos, the "ally" of Odysseus. Likewise, as Odysseus' principal rival was the suitor Antinous, thus this contrast could allude to not only Homer's poem, but to the Hermetic connection between Antinous and Arcadia as well.[22] There is a further allusion in the poem from Oxyrhynchus, which says that Antinous rode a horse that was "swifter than the horse of Adrastus."[23] In his excellent study on the Greek cult of Pan, Philippe Borgeaud relates an Arcadian myth in which Poseidon and Demeter give birth to the horse Areion, who was the horse of Adrastus.[24] Antinous is connected with horses elsewhere in poetry,[25] and in an issue of several Arcadian coins by one Veturius, Antinous is on the obverse side and a horse is on the reverse.[26] Antinous was being woven into extant Arcadian myths, including that of Pan, through these means.

Antinous is given a parallel myth to one relating to Pan in a further poem from Oxyrhynchus, which is securely dated to the late third century CE. In Virgil's *Georgics* 3.383-393, Pan is said to have lured Selene, the moon goddess, to the woods through his wiles to be his lover.[27] In the third-century hymn that mentions Antinous from Egypt, it states likewise that Selene "upon more brilliant hopes bade [Antinous] shine as a star-like bridegroom and garlanding the new light with a circle she took him for her husband."[28] Antinous' association with the moon according to the 2nd century CE Christian writer Tatian the Assyrian,[29] therefore, may be confirmed by this particular later source; but, in a sense, the Arcadian connection is also furthered by it, since the Arcadians were said to be *proselenoi*, as mentioned previously.

However, it is in the realm of numismatics where Antinous and Pan's connection is really made explicit. In several unprovenanced coins, Antinous is portrayed on the obverse side of the coin with Pan on the reverse, or he is portrayed with the *pedum* (the curved shepherd's staff that was an attribute of Pan) on his shoulder, with a coin legend reading "Antinous Pan."[30] In an issue of contorniate medallions featuring Antinous on the obverse and either a bull or a winged Victoria Augusta on the reverse, likewise Antinous is portrayed with the *pedum* and the inscription indicates this is Antinous Pan.[31] A papyrus scrap containing a short note from Oxyrhynchus also indicates a close connection between Antinous and Pan in at least one no-longer-extant iconographic instance, in which a "public boat whose emblem is Panantinous" is mentioned as the ship via which the business transaction noted is to take place.[32] While this is novel in the Egyptian context, the syncretism is far from unheard of, contrary to what J. E. G. Whitehorne says on the matter,[33] particularly in light of the numistmatic examples mentioned here. However, he is correct to point out the connection of Antinous to the Nile and Pan as a protector of travelers as a possible reason why such an emblem would be desirable for a ship on the Nile.[34]

A final interesting instance of Pan syncretism occurs in an iconographic context in relation to Antinous. At Lanuvium near Rome, Antinous and Diana shared a temple that was maintained by a *collegium*,[35] and separate from that temple an image of Antinous as Silvanus was discovered.[36] Pan and Silvanus have a great deal of overlap in their associations, including homoerotic connections;[37] however, the usual Roman syncretism or equivalent of Pan is Faunus, who is occasionally syncretized to or confused with Silvanus.[38] On the Arch of Constantine in Rome, there are eight *tondi* depicting hunting scenes with sacrifices to particular deities made before (or after) them, which were originally from a Hadrianic hunting monument. At least one of these depicts Antinous, though two more do so conjecturally.[39] On one of the scenes a sacrifice to a deity that used to be identified as Silvanus is depicted, but which Peter Dorcey conjectures is more likely to be a syncretic form of Pan-Silvanus.[40] Hadrian's reign was one of the few in which Silvanus seems to have had any depictions that were direct imperial sanctions, with this instance and others among them, as well as Hadrian's memorial arch for Trajan, and then Antoninus Pius (Hadrian's successor) issuing a coin for the apotheosis of Hadrian which had Silvanus on the reverse.[41] The emperor was known to have enjoyed hunting a great deal,[42] and so Silvanus would have been a most appropriate deity to have patronized this activity; but, Pan would have been equally so.

It is impossible to account for a systematic program of syncretism with the ancient cultus of Antinous,[43] though certain patterns certainly emerge. In the Arcadian cultus of Antinous in Mantineia, his connection to the Arcadian ethnicity is established and emphasized; the same is true of several occurrences of his cultus in Egypt in their wider associations. The connection of Antinous to hunting is also something that was supported on the direct imperial level, as concluded from the evidence which is available to us. And, a connection to Hermes was often part and parcel of various Antinoan cult remains. All of these factors make the syncretism between Antinous and Pan, as well as the variety of other connections between them, both logical and expectable. The eroticism of Pan — whether homoerotic or along more conventional lines — was furthered through his connection to Antinous, and through the adaptation of Antinous' myths from the model established by Pan. Both Pan and Antinous were able to express their love of their devotees through common cultic, mythic, and iconographic identifications, and that love was particularly and explicitly an Arcadian form of love.

Notes

[1] Philippe Borgeaud, *The Cult of Pan in Ancient Greece*, trans. Kathleen Atlass and James Redfield (Chicago and London: University of Chicago Press, 1988), p. 3.

[2] See Phillip A. Bernhardt-House, *Werewolves, Magical Hounds and Dog-Headed Men in Celtic Literature* (Lewiston, NY: The Edwin Mellen Press, 2010), pp. 144-147, for further detailed references on these traditions.

[3] Borgeaud, pp. 6-7.

[4] Borgeaud, p. 4.

[5] Borgeaud, p. 75, 221 note 11; Bernard Sargent, *Homosexuality in Greek Myth*, trans. Arthur Goldhammer (Boston: Beacon Press, 1986), pp. 259-260. Further, Walter Burkert, *Homo Necans: The Anthropology of Ancient Greek Sacrificial Ritual and Myth*, trans. Peter Bing (Berkeley and Los Angeles: University of California Press, 1983), pp. 112-114, connects the cave of Cheiron and Pan's cultus there to the werewolf rituals of Mt. Lykaion.

[6] Randy P. Conner, David Hatfield Sparks and Mariya Sparks (eds.), *Cassells' Encyclopedia of Queer Myth, Symbol and Spirit* (London and New York: Cassell, 1997), pp. 66-67 s.v. Arcadia. A modern Uranian story that likewise connects Pan to homoeroticism is Forrest Reid, *The Garden God: A Tale of Two Boys*, ed. Michael Matthew Kaylor (Kansas City: Valancourt Books, 2007).

[7] W. H. S. Jones (ed./trans.), Pausanias, *Description of Greece*, Volume 3 (Cambridge: Harvard University Press, 1933), pp. 380-383.

[8] Jones, pp. 388-389; Jennifer Larson, *Greek Heroine Cults* (Madison: University of Wisconsin Press, 1995), pp. 10, 144, 162n30.

[9] Jones, pp. 386-389.

[10] Jones, pp. 388-391.

[11] Jones, pp. 384-387.

[12] Jones, pp. 390-393.

[13] Jones, pp. 390-391.

[14] Royston Lambert, *Beloved and God: The Story of Hadrian and Antinous* (New York: Viking, 1984), p. 191; Anthony R. Birley, *Hadrian the Restless Emperor* (London: Routledge, 2000), p. 180; Hugo Meyer, Antinoos: Die archäologischen Denkmäler unter Einbeziehung des numismatischen und epigraphischen Materials sowie der literarischen Nachrichten, Ein Beitrag zur Kunst- und Kulturgeschichte der hadrianisch-frühantoninischen Zeit (Munich: Wilhelm Fink, 1991), p. 200. Further inscriptions commemorate Antinous in Mantineia,

including Meyer, p. 125, which may be by Antinous' mother and father, though Caroline Vout disputes this—Caroline Vout, Power and Eroticism in Imperial Rome (Cambridge: Cambridge University Press, 2007), p. 131n160; and one by Epitynchanus and Doxa for their son Isochrysus, who in death is entrusted to Antinous' protection, Vout, p. 123n37.

[15] Even in Antinoöpolis, the city founded in Egypt in Antinous' honor, there is a distinctly Arcadian association attached to him. The phyla of Antinoöpolis named for Antinous, Oseirantinoeioi (Osiris-Antinous), has three demoi in it with Arcadian connections: Hermaieus (after Hermes, one of Arcadia's principal gods), Kleitorios and Parrhasios (both Arcadian heroes who were the offspring of either Lykaion or Arkas); Mary Taliafero Boatwright, *Hadrian and the Cities of Rome* (Princeton: Princeton University Press, 2000), p. 194n124.

[16] Wolfgang Dieter Lebek, "Ein Hymnus auf Antinoos," Zeitschrift für Papyrologie und Epigraphik 12.2 (1973), pp. 101-137 at 109.

[17] Birley, pp. 252-253.

[18] Arthur S. Hunt (ed.), *The Oxyrhynchus Papyri 8* (London: Egypt Exploration Society, 1911), pp. 73-77 at 75.

[19] Meyer, pp. 170-171.

[20] Sir James George Frazer (trans.), Apollodorus, *The Library*, 2 Volumes (Cambridge: Harvard University Press, 1921), Vol. 2, pp. 304-305 (Epitome vii.38).

[21] Richmond Lattimore (trans.), *The Odyssey of Homer* (New York: Harper Perennial, 1991), pp. 260-261 (17.290-327).

[22] The Hermetic connection within Egypt is also emphasized by both J. R. Rea and Caroline Vout, who remind us that Antinous died within the Hermopolite nome, and that Antinoöpolis was just across the Nile from Hermopolis, which (apart from the Arcadian connection) may give part of the justification for the insistent Hermetic connection between Antinous and Hermes; J. R. Rea (ed.), *The Oxyrhynchus Papyri 63* (London: Egypt Exploration Society, 1996), p. 10; Vout, p. 132n176.

[23] Hunt, p. 75.

[24] Borgeaud, p. 57.

[25] Vout, p. 122n20.

[26] Gustave Blum, "Numismatique d'Antinoos," *Journal International d"Archéologie Numismatique* 16 (1914), pp. 33-70 at 37-38.

[27] H. Rushton Fairclough (trans.), Virgil, *Eclogues, Georgics, Aeneid I-VI* (Cambridge: Harvard University Press, 1935), pp. 180-183.

[28] Rea, p. 10.

[29] See my article in Thista Minai et al. (eds.), *Unbound: A Devotional*

Anthology for Artemis (Eugene: Bibliotheca Alexandrina, 2008), pp. 106-112 at 110.

[30] Blum, p. 57, plate IV, 13-14.

[31] Blum, p. 57, plate V, 13-14. On the contorniate medals of Antinous, see also Elisabeth Alföldi-Rosenbaum, "Hadrian and Antinous on the Contorniates and in the Vita Hadriani," in Giorgio Bonamente and Noël Duval (eds.), *Historiae Augustae Colloquium Parisinum* (Macerata: Universita degli Studi di Macerata, 1991), pp. 11-18.

[32] E. W. Handley, H. G. Ioannidou, P. J. Parsons, and J. E. G. Whitehorne (eds.), *The Oxyrhynchus Papyri 59* (1992), pp. 99-101 at 100.

[33] Handley, Ioannidou, Parsons and Whitehorne, p. 101.

[34] Handley, Ioannidou, Parsons and Whitehorne, p. 101. However, both Whitehorne and Blum, p. 70, make the point that Antinous' frequent Hermetic syncretism would also cover this travel-protection aspect, and that the Hermetic connection is much more widespread.

[35] Mary Beard, John North, and Simon Price (eds./trans.), *Religions of Rome*, Volume 2: A Sourcebook (Cambridge: Cambridge University Press, 1998), pp. 292-294.

[36] Peter F. Dorcey, *The Cult of Silvanus: A Study in Roman Folk Religion* (Leiden: E. J. Brill, 1992), pp. 100-102. This relief is depicted on the Neos Alexandria website's temple page for Antinous.

[37] Dorcey, p. 38n19.

[38] Dorcey, pp. 33-48.

[39] Mary Taliafero Boatwright, *Hadrian and the City of Rome* (Princeton: Princeton University Press, 1987), pp. 190-202.

[40] Dorcey, pp. 98-100.

[41] Dorcey, pp. 96-98.

[42] Birley, passim.

[43] I would note that cultus in Latin is a fourth declension masculine noun, which means that it has the same morphology in the nominative singular and nominative plural. Few of the cults to deities in the ancient world truly had a scope much wider than their individual local forms, despite the fact that many shared a deity across their widespread localities.

Lament at Banias

Diotima Sophia

They come to see
        The touch of the god
                Beside the cave and fire
The bring their gifts
        Of sacrifice
                They bring their staid desires

"A working hand" "A mended back"
        "My legs be strong and true"
And these I grant
        But more, I crave
                The few ...

Who know the cost
        And count it dear
But balk not at the price

For what I would heal
        Is humanity

Come – let me show you – life

A life well-lived
        In joy and pain
                Throw off the binding chains

Throw off the rules
        Throw off the thoughts
                Till only – you – remain

Be mad with me
        And dance, and leap

By Panic, be you found
The goat-foot god
　　The healing god
　　　　Pipes a maenad sound

Be healed
　　If you will
　　If that will satisfy

But for those of you
　　For those fair few
　　Who grasp the wings to fly

Seek healing not
　　But brokenness
　　And Panic – pain, and strife
For only then
　　And only so
　　　　Will you understand this life

Saltless meat
　　Is thin, sour wine
　　The spice, is food indeed
Come dance with me
　　Says the goat foot god
　　As he plays upon the reed

The great god Pan they called me then
　　And feared, themselves, to be...

There are few who may
　　Fewer still, who will

Now come – will you – dance with me?

Author Biographies

Amanda Sioux Blake is the keeper of the Temple of Athena the Savior, Alexandrian Tradition. She is the author of *Ink In My Veins: A Collection of Contemporary Pagan Poetry*, and *Songs of Praise: Hymns to the Gods of Greece*, as well as the forthcoming *Doing Ma'at: A Short Primer on Greco-Egyptian Ethics* and *Journey to Olympos: A Modern Spiritual Odyssey*.

A self-labeled history geek, she has taught classes on Greek Mythology and contacting your spirit guides at her local chapter of Spiritual Frontiers Fellowship International. She is currently teaching "Olympos in Egypt," an introduction to the unique hybrid culture and spiritually that grew up in Alexandria, Egypt in the Hellenistic Age, sponsored by the Temple. If you are interested, visit templeofathena.wordpress.com, or email her at starsong_dragon @yahoo.com. She also runs Otherworld Creations, an online store specializing in Pagan and fantasy designs, at cafepress.com/other_world.

Christa A. Bergerson has been worshipping and adoring the wondrous Roman-Greco-Egyptian Gods since she was a precocious tot. She is also an occultist, an environmentalist, and a Guardian of those who writhe betwixt the veil. In her spare time, she enjoys listening to phonographs, traversing the sparse wilds of Illinois, and swimming in the dead of night. Her intuited poetry has appeared in *Waters of Life*, *Bearing Torches*, *The Beltane Papers*, *Sex and Murder*, *The Nocturnal Lyric*, and *Faerie Nation Magazine*, among other publications. For astral and/or sublunary communication feel free to visit her at carmentaeternus.com.

Rebecca Buchanan is the Editor-in-Chief of Bibliotheca Alexandrina. She is also the editor of *Eternal Haunted Summer*, a Pagan literary ezine. She has been previously published in *Datura: An Anthology of Esoteric Poesis* (Scarlet Imprint); *Into the Great Below: A Devotional to Inanna and Ereshkigal* (Asphodel Press); *Luna Station Quarterly*; *Cliterature*; and in other venues.

Dr Dave Evans is a historian of British social culture in general and of British postwar occultism in particular, being the author of *History of British Magick after Crowley* (Hidden, 2007), and contributor to numerous websites, magazines and books. He can be contacted via daveevansuk.reachby.com.

Tabitha Few grew up in southern Illinois and currently lives close to Chicago, Illinois in a small apartment with her love, Jason and their pet plant, Audrey. Tabitha does not consider herself a Hellenic polytheist, but she does have a self-proclaimed god crush on Pan. When she isn't busy taking care of her love, Tabitha enjoys creative projects, such as drawing, sculpting, and writing, but seldom considers her work to be very good. Jason heartily disagrees.

Jason Ross Inczauskis is a graduate student residing close to Chicago, Illinois, living in a small apartment with his love, Tabitha, his pet plant, Audrey the Immortal, and more books than you can shake a stick at. He is a fairly recent convert to Hellenismos despite a long-held fascination with the Greek Gods. When asked about his spiritual path, he may refer to himself as a Hellene, a Hellenic, or Greek Pre-Orthodox, depending on who's asking and his mood at the time, though he always follows it with the caveat: 'but not a very good one.' He has worshipped Athena for many years, but now honors the other Hellenic deities as well.

Galina Krasskova is an ardent devotee of Odin and has been a priest since 1995. She is a Northern Tradition Shaman, whose primary focus is encouraging and developing a tradition of Heathen devotional work. She is the author of several books including *Exploring the Northern Tradition*, *The Whisperings of Woden*, and *Sigyn: Our Lady of the Staying Power*. Krasskova is currently at work on a devotional for Kali (she owes Her a debt). She holds a diploma in interfaith ministry, a Masters degree in religious studies and lectures frequently throughout the US.

Leafshimmer is an Initiate of the Anderson Feri (Faery) Tradition. He is also a High Priest (Minos) of the Minoan Brotherhood. Shimmer has led several semi-public Pagan rituals, mostly in Radical Faerie contexts, and has invoked Pan at a number of these. Io Pan!

P. Sufenas Virius Lupus is a founding member of the Ekklesía Antínoou (a queer, Graeco-Roman-Egyptian syncretist reconstructionist polytheist religious group dedicated to Antinous, the deified lover of the Roman Emperor Hadrian and other related gods and divine figures), a contributing member of Neos Alexandria, and a Celtic Reconstructionist pagan. You can find Lupus' work published in the Bibliotheca Alexandrina volumes dedicated to Hekate, Isis and Serapis, and Artemis, with upcoming writings and poems in the devotionals to Zeus and the Dioskouroi. Lupus has published a book of poems, *The Phillupic Hymns* (2008), a further book called *The Syncretisms of Antinous* (2010), and also has poems printed in the Scarlet Imprint anthology *Datura: An Anthology of Esoteric Poesis* (2010). You can find Lupus' blog at aediculaantinoi.wordpress.com.

Kenn Payne is a freelance writer, poet and practising pagan of over ten years. After finding Hellenismos in 2003, he has nurtured relationships with Hekate, Dionysos, Aphrodite and Pan. He has previously been published in the BA titles *Unbound: A Devotional Anthology for Artemis* and *Bearing Torches: A Devotional Anthology for Hekate*.

Diana Rajchel lives, works, writes, perfumes, dances and cultivates in urban Minneapolis. She shares her experiences with her husband, two robots and dear friends. If you'd like to read more of her work, you can find it at dianarajchel.com

Michael Routery is a writer and poet living in San Francisco, whose work has appeared in a wide variety of publications, including *Beatitude 50*, *Datura*, and the Bibliotheca Alexandrina devotional anthologies *Written in Wine*, *Bearing Torches*, and *Unbound*. A long time pagan and Dionysian, he belongs to the Neo-Druidic fellowship FoDLA, and the Ekklesía Antínoou. He can be found online at finnchuill.livejournal.com.

Diotima Sophia may not be the original Diotima, but the author does agree that the western world has invested far too much energy into separating the inseparable duo of mind and heart. Diotima has written widely on a number of subjects, including essays, fiction and poetry.

Her two latest books have been published by the Bibliotheca Alexandrina: *Dancing God* – a collection of poetry – and *The Goat Foot God*, an examination of the Great God Pan; both available through Neos Alexandria.

Select Bibliography

Primary Sources

(Homer). "The Homeric Hymn to Hermes." from
  http://ancienthistory.about.com/library/bl/bl_text_homerhymn_hermes.htm.
(Homer). "The Homeric Hymn to Pan." from
  http://ancienthistory.about.com/library/bl/bl_text_homerhymn_pan.htm.
Aeschylus. "Eumenides." from
  http://classics.mit.edu/Aeschylus/eumendides.html.
Apollonius Rhodius. Argonautica.
Aristophanes. (1938). "Women at the Thesmophoria." Translator: Eugene O'Neill. Retrieved 4.6.06.
Callimachus. "Hymn III: To Artemis." from
  http://www.chss.montclair.edu/classics/HYMNART.HTML.
Chrysostom, D. "Discourses: The Sixth Discourse: Diogenes, or On Tyranny ", from
  "http://penelope.uchicago.edu/Thayer/E/Roman/Texts/Dio_Chrysostom/Discourses/6*.html"
Euripides. (1850). "Bacchae." The Tragedies of Euripides, translated by T. A. Buckley.
  http://perseus.uchicago.edu/hopper/toc.jsp?doc=Perseus:text:1999.01.0092:card=945.
Frazer, A. J. G. (2008). *Apollodorus: The Library*, Bibliobazaar.
Habicht, C. (1998). *Pausanius' Guide to Ancient Greece*, Univ of California Pr.
Hall, E. (1997). *Aeschylus' Persians*, Aris & Phillips.
Hesiod (1999). *Theogony*, Oxford, Oxford Paperbacks.
Hyginus. "Fabulae 191." from
  http://www.theoi.com/Text/HyginusFabulae4.html.
Morgan, J. R. (2004). Longus. *Daphnis and Chloe*, Oxford: Aris & Phillips.
Mynors, R. A. B. and P. V. Maro (1994). Virgil, *Georgics*, Clarendon Press.

Nonnus. "Dionysiaca I." from
   http://www.theoi.com/Text/NonnusDionysiacaI.html.
Ovid (1955). *Metamorphoses*, London, Penguin.
Pindar. *Hymn to Pan*.
Theocritus. "Idyll VII." from
   http://www.theoi.com/Text/TheocritusIdylls2.html.

Books for Children and Teens

D'Aulaire, I. and E. P. D'Aulaire (1993). *d'Aulaire's Book of Greek Myths*. Huntington Beach, Teacher Created Materials, Inc.
Grahame, K. (1917). "The wind in the willows."
   http://etext.virginia.edu/toc/modeng/public/GraWind.html.
Napoli, D. J. (2003). *The Great God Pan*, Random/Wendy Lamb Books.
Riordan, Rick. *Percy Jackson and the Olympians*, Puffin Books
Siekkinen, R. (1990). *The Curious Faun*, Carolrhoda Books.

Secondary Sources

Barrett Browning, E. (1900a). "The Dead Pan." *The Complete Poetical Works*, Cambridge ed. Boston, Houghton, Mifflin.
Barrett Browning, E. (1900b). "A Musical Instrument." *The Complete Poetical Works*, Cambridge ed. Boston, Houghton, Mifflin.
Boardman, J. (1997). *The Great God Pan: The Survival of an Image*, London, Thames and Hudson.
Borgeaud, P. (1983). "The Death of the Great Pan: The Problem of Interpretation." *History of Religions* 22(3): 254- 283
Browning, R. (1981). Pan and Luna. *Robert Browning: The Poems*. J. Pettigrew and T. J. Collins. New Haven, Yale Univ. Press. 2
Burkert, W. (1985). *Greek Religion*, Oxford, Blackwell.
Diotima (2008). *The Goat Foot God*, Bibliotheca Alexandrina.
Dunsany, L. (2003). *The Blessing of Pan*, Wildside Press.
Hawthorne, N. "The Marble Faun." from "http://www.online-literature.com/hawthorne/marble_faun/
Hillman, J. and W. Roscher (1972). *Pan and the Nightmare: Two Essays*, Woodstock, CT, Spring.

Larson, J. L. (2001). *Greek Nymphs: Myth, Cult, Lore*, Oxford University Press, USA.

Machen, A. (1894). "The Great God Pan." Retrieved 29.5.06, from http://www.gutenberg.org/dirs/etext96/ggpan10.txt.

Mallarmé, S. (1882). *L'Après-midi d'un faune*, La Revue indépendante.

Merivale, P. (1991). "The Cult of Pan in Ancient Greece." *The Journal of Americam Folklore* 104(413): 390 - 382

Milton, J. (2003). "On the Morning of Christ's Nativity." *Complete Poems and Major Prose,* Hackett Publishing.

Mynors, R. A. B. and P. V. Maro (1994). Virgil, *Georgics*, Clarendon Press.

Vinci, L. (1993). *Pan - Great God of Nature*. London, Neptune Press.

Walter, Hans. *Pan's Returns: The God of the Greek Wilderness*

West, M. L. (1983). *The Orphic Poems*, Oxford University Press, USA.

Wilson, J. F. (2004). *Caesarea Philippi: Banias, The Lost City of Pan*, IB Tauris.

About the Bibliotheca Alexandrina

Ptolemy Soter, the first Makedonian ruler of Egypt, established the library at Alexandria to collect all of the world's learning in a single place. His scholars compiled definitive editions of the Classics, translated important foreign texts into Greek, and made monumental strides in science, mathematics, philosophy and literature. By some accounts over a million scrolls were housed in the famed library, and though it has long since perished due to the ravages of war, fire, and human ignorance, the image of this great institution has remained as a powerful inspiration down through the centuries.

To help promote the revival of traditional polytheistic religions we have launched a series of books dedicated to the ancient gods of Greece and Egypt. The library is a collaborative effort drawing on the combined resources of the different elements within the modern Hellenic and Kemetic communities, in the hope that we can come together to praise our gods and share our diverse understandings, experiences and approaches to the divine.

A list of our current and forthcoming titles can be found on the following page. For more information on the Bibliotheca, our submission requirements for upcoming devotionals, or to learn about our organization, please visit us at *www.neosalexandria.org*.

Sincerely,

The Editorial Board of the Library of Neos Alexandria

Current Titles from the Bibliotheca Alexandrina:

Written in Wine: A Devotional Anthology for Dionysos
Dancing God: Poetry of Myths and Magicks by Diotima
Goat Foot God by Diotima
Longing for Wisdom: The Message of the Maxims by Allyson Szabo
The Phillupic Hymns by P. Sufenas Virius Lupus
Unbound: A Devotional Anthology for Artemis
Waters of Life: A Devotional Anthology for Isis and Serapis
Bearing Torches: A Devotional Anthology for Hekate
Queen of the Great Below: An Anthology in Honor of Ereshkigal
From Cave to Sky: A Devotional Anthology in Honor of Zeus
Out of Arcadia: A Devotional Anthology in Honor of Pan

Forthcoming Titles from the Bibliotheca Alexandrina:

Megaloi Theoi: A Devotional in Honor of The Dioskouroi and Their Family
Anointed: A Devotional in Honor of the Deities of the Near and Middle East
The Scribing Ibis: An Anthology of Pagan Fiction in Honor of Thoth
Queen of the Sacred Way: A Devotional Anthology in Honor of Persephone

Printed in Great Britain
by Amazon